S. Russell Forbes

The Footsteps of St. Paul in Rome

An historical memoir from the apostles landing at Puteoli to his death -

A.D. 62-64

S. Russell Forbes

The Footsteps of St. Paul in Rome
An historical memoir from the apostles landing at Puteoli to his death - A.D. 62-64

ISBN/EAN: 9783337381158

Printed in Europe, USA, Canada, Australia, Japan

Cover: Foto ©ninafisch / pixelio.de

More available books at **www.hansebooks.com**

THE FOOTSTEPS OF ST. PAUL IN ROME

An Historical Memoir
FROM THE APOSTLE'S LANDING AT PUTEOLI TO HIS DEATH
A.D. 62-64

BY

S. RUSSELL FORBES, PH.D.
Archæological and Historical Lecturer on the Roman Antiquities;
AUTHOR OF "RAMBLES IN ROME," ETC.

ST. PAUL.
(From a Glass Vase, fifth Century.)

4th EDITION, REVISED AND ENLARGED.

"I am ready to preach the gospel to you that are at Rome also."
Romans i. 15.

THOMAS NELSON AND SONS,
London, Edinburgh, and New York.

ROME: S. R. FORBES, 76 VIA DELLA CROCE.

Preface to the Fourth Edition.

AS the interest in the Footsteps of the great Apostle to the Gentiles in Rome continues to increase, so are we happily able to add some new discovery and detail to our Historical Memoir as each edition is called for. The recent explorations and discoveries in the House and Church of Pudens, the re-opening of the Platonia, where his body rested, on the Appian Way, and the new details concerning his actual tomb, all tend to enhance this little book of historical facts.

It is highly gratifying to us to know that our efforts in making his footsteps plain have met with much appreciation.

S. R. F.

ROME, *St. Paul's Day, June 29, 1897.*

Contents.

I. PORTRAIT OF ST. PAUL,	9
II. THE TRAVELS OF ST. PAUL,	10
III. THE ROAD TO ROME,	16
IV. ROMANUS SUM,	30
V. THE EARLY CHURCH IN ROME,	39
VI. THE BRITISH ROYAL FAMILY, ST. PAUL, PUDENS, AND MARTIAL,	44
VII. WORK AND DEATH,	53
VIII. A SILENT WITNESS,	62
IX. ST. PAUL'S EPISTLES FROM ROME,	63
X. TRES TABERNÆ: A TOPOGRAPHICAL STUDY,	75

APPENDIX,	79
WAS ST. PETER EVER IN ROME?	84
THE CHRISTIAN EMPEROR,	80
THE EARLY BRITISH CHURCH,	92

List of Illustrations.

PORTRAITS OF SS. PAUL AND PETER,	*Frontispiece*
PORTRAIT OF ST. PAUL,	*Title*
MAP OF ST. PAUL'S TRAVELS,	8
ST. PAUL'S LANDING-PLACE AT PUTEOLI,	17
TOMB OF CECILIA METELLA,	23
CLAUDIAN AQUEDUCT,	24
ARCH OF DRUSUS,	25
MAP OF ANCIENT ROME,	29
THE FORUM IN ST. PAUL'S DAY,	31
THE CIRCUS MAXIMUS,	53
PORTRAITS OF NERO AND POPPÆA,	59
ST. PETER'S, AND OBELISK,	62

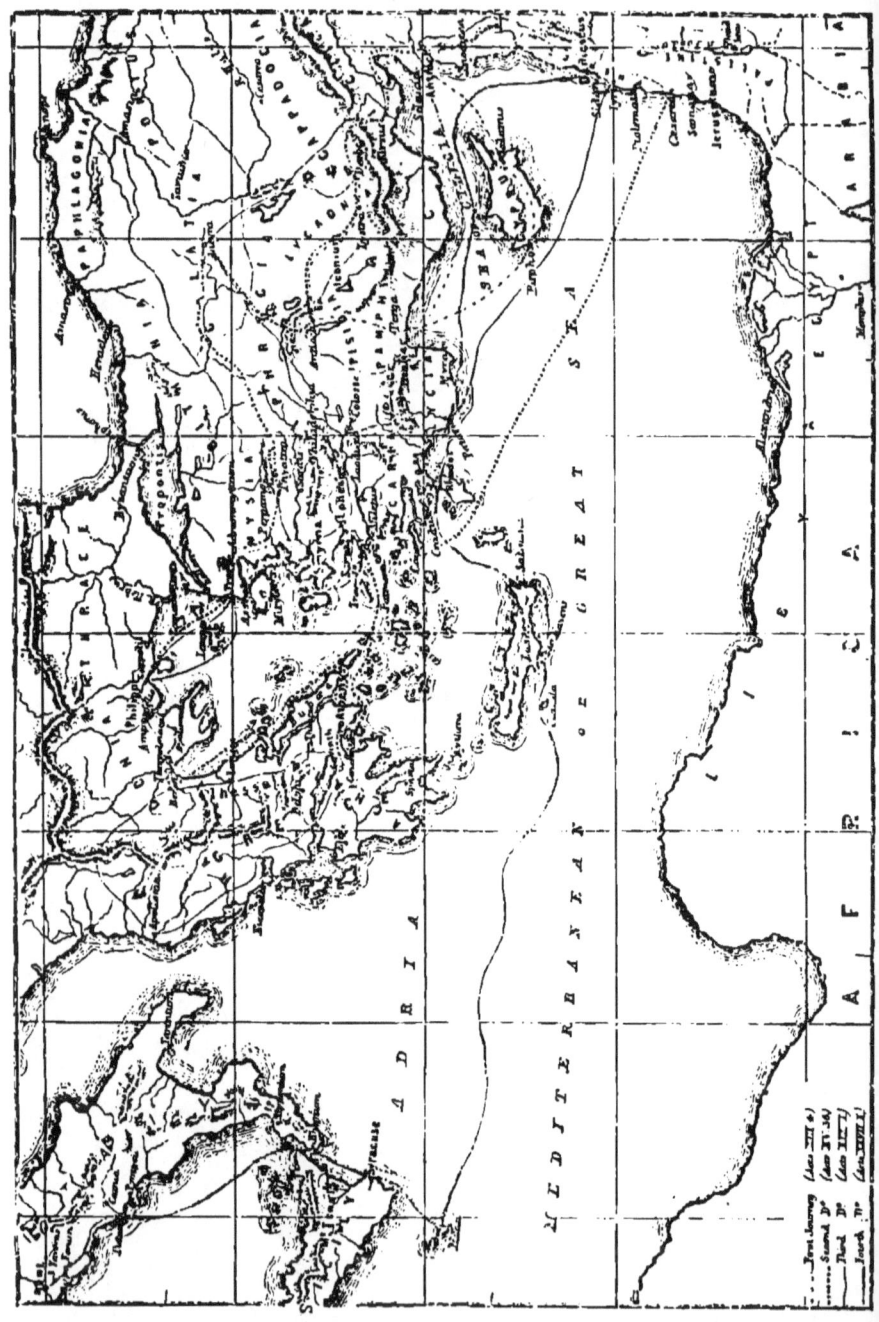

THE FOOTSTEPS OF ST. PAUL IN ROME.

I.

PORTRAIT OF ST. PAUL.

AMONGST the many objects of interest found in the Catacombs have been the gilt glass vases representing the heads of some of the apostles and saints, and also pagan subjects. The dates of these vases are arrived at by comparing them with the dated mosaic pictures and artistic details which are known to have been introduced at certain periods: for example, the *labarum* of Constantine and the ☧, neither of which was used before the fourth century.

The head of St. Paul, of which we give a facsimile, was found in the Catacombs (which, is not known), and is preserved in the Vatican Library. It has the word PAVLVS over the head, so there is no doubt as to whom it represents. It is of the fifth century, and very similar to others where he is represented with St. Peter. He is always shown as having a bald head, whilst St. Peter has plenty of hair, as in the preceding portraits, where both are shown together as they appear on a bronze medal found in the Catacombs of Domitilla, and which medal is probably of the fourth century. By means of these portraits we are enabled to form some idea of the likenesses of these two saints; which portraits were most likely taken from contemporary ones, or from traditions handing down their appearance. They are undoubtedly the oldest portraits of SS. Paul and Peter. Eusebius ("E. H.," vii. 18) says:—"Since we have also seen representations of the apostles Peter and Paul, and of Christ himself, still preserved in paintings."

II.

THE TRAVELS OF ST. PAUL.

FIRST TOUR.

A.D. 36. SAUL is present at the death of Stephen.

37. On a journey to Damascus is converted (Acts ix. 2, xxii. 6, xxvi. 12).

He goes to Arabia (Gal. i. 17). Returns to Damascus, and escapes from there by being let down from a window in a basket (2 Cor. xi. 33).

40. Easter. Three years after his conversion he went to Jerusalem (Gal. i. 18), tarried there fifteen days, then "the brethren brought him down to Cæsarea, and sent him forth to Tarsus," his native city (Acts ix. 30).

"Afterwards I came into the regions of Syria and Cilicia" (Gal. i. 21).

Barnabas went to Tarsus to seek Saul (Acts xi. 25), and brought him unto Antioch in Syria, and stayed there one year. And there the disciples were first called Christians (43 A.D.). St. Luke was a native of Antioch.

43. Barnabas and Saul sent to Jerusalem (Acts xi. 30). Return to Antioch with John Mark, nephew of Barnabas (xii. 25).

45. They went down to Seleucia, and thence sailed to Cyprus (xiii. 4), and landed at Salamis, crossing to Paphos (xiii. 5, 6).

The proconsul Sergius Paulus converted. Saul assumes the name of Paul.

Sailing to Perga in Pamphylia, John returning to Jerusalem, they came to Antioch in Pisidia (xiii. 14). "But they shook off the dust of their feet against them, and came unto Iconium" (xiii. 51). "Long time therefore they tarried there" (xiv. 3). Disturbances arising, they fled to Lystra and Derbe, cities of Lycaonia (xiv. 5, 6), where they were called Jupiter and Mercury. Paul is stoned (xiv. 19). He goes with Barnabas to Derbe (xiv. 20). Return by Lystra and Iconium to Antioch (xiv. 21). Pass through Pisidia to Pamphylia (xiv. 24).

48. Preach in Perga, and went down into Attalia (xiv. 25). Sail to Antioch of Syria (xiv. 26), "and there they abode long time with the disciples" (xiv. 28).

SECOND TOUR.

A.D. 50. Fourteen years after Paul's conversion he goes to Jerusalem with Barnabas and Titus (Gal. ii. 1).
Paul and Barnabas start for Jerusalem (Acts xv. 2). Pass through Phenice and Samaria.
The elders write letters, and send Judas (Barsabas) and Silas, with Paul and Barnabas, back to Antioch (xv. 22).
Peter goes to Antioch. Paul withstands him to the face (Gal. ii. 11).
Paul and Silas go through Syria and Cilicia (Acts xv. 41).
Timotheus ("our brother") converted at Lystra (xvi. 1).
51. They went throughout Phrygia and the region of Galatia. Came to Mysia, and down to Troas (xvi. 8). Here he is joined by Luke, and they sail to Samothracia, Neapolis, Philippi in Macedonia (xvi. 12). Scourged, imprisoned, and put in the stocks (xvi. 24; 1 Thess. ii. 2). Earthquake (xvi. 26), convert jailer (34), claim to be Romans (37), depart (40). Pass through Amphipolis and Apollonia to— *In Europe.*
52. Thessalonica (xvii. 1; 1 Thess. ii. 9; 2 Thess. ii. 5). A riot is raised, and they go to Berea (Acts xvii. 10). Paul sails to Athens, leaving Silas and Timotheus behind (ver. 14; 1 Thess. iii. 1) to go to Thessalonica (1 Thess. iii. 2). Preaches on Mars' Hill. Paul departs from Athens and comes to Corinth (xviii. 1; 1 Cor. ii. 1–4, xv. 1; 2 Cor. xi. 9). Stays at house of Gaius (Rom. xvi. 23; 1 Thess. iii. 6). Finds Aquila and Priscilla there (Acts xviii. 2). Silas and Timotheus join him (ver. 5).
53. He continued there a year and a half (ver. 11), and it was during this time probably that he visited Illyricum: "I have fully preached the gospel of Christ unto Illyricum" (Rom. xv. 19). Writes his first epistle to the Thessalonians, and sends Timotheus with it (1 Thess. iii. 2). Brought before Gallio the proconsul, brother of Seneca (Acts xviii. 12). "After this he tarried there yet a good while" (18). Writes second epistle to the Thessalonians. *Writes First to Thessalonians.* *Writes Second to Thessalonians.*
Sailed to Syria, visiting Cenchrea (where he shaved his head) and Ephesus on his way (xviii. 19). Landed at Cæsarea in Palestine, went up to Jerusalem, and then down to Antioch (22).

THIRD TOUR

After some time passed at Antioch, Paul "went over all the country of Galatia and Phrygia in order" (Acts xviii. 23).

A.D. 56. "Paul having passed through the upper coasts came to Ephesus" (Acts xix. 1). He stayed there three months disputing in the synagogue (ver. 8), and then in the school of one Tyrannus for the space of two years.

58. Sending Timotheus and Erastus into Macedonia, he himself stayed in Asia for a season. Writes his first epistle to the Corinthians, in which he says, "I will tarry at Ephesus until Pentecost" (1 Cor. xvi. 8), and sends Timothy (1 Cor. iv. 17) and Titus with it (2 Cor. viii. 6, xii. 18). At length a riot was raised by Demetrius (Acts xix. 23; 2 Cor. i. 8), and he departed for Macedonia (Acts xx. 1; 1 Tim. i. 3). He takes Troas on his way, expecting to find Titus there; but not finding him, he goes into Macedonia (2 Cor. ii. 13). "When we had come to Macedonia, God comforted us by the coming of Titus" (2 Cor. vii. 6). They probably met at Philippi, where St. Paul would write his second epistle to the Corinthians, which he sends by Titus, Luke (2 Cor. viii. 18), and Timotheus (22). "To spare you came I not as yet to Corinth" (2 Cor. i. 23). "And when he had gone over those parts, he came into Greece, and there abode three months" (Acts xx. 2, 3). At this time he must have paid his promised and deferred visit to Corinth, staying at the house of Gaius (1 Cor. xvi. 2, 3, 5; 2 Cor. i. 16, xiii. 1). Here he writes his epistles to the Romans and Galatians (Rom. xvi. 23), and then leaves for Jerusalem (Rom. xv. 25; Acts xxiv. 17).

Writes First to Corinthians.

Writes Second to Corinthians.

Writes to the Romans and Galatians.

59. He returned through Macedonia into Asia (Acts xx. 3). "We sailed from the port of Philippi and came to Troas, where we abode seven days" (6). Here, walking on foot to Assos, he left his cloak and parchments, which later on he asks Timothy to bring with him to Rome (2 Tim. iv. 13). The company sail to Assos, but Paul goes on foot (Acts xx. 13), and sails thence with the brethren to Mitylene (14); then by Chios, Samos, and tarry at Trogyllium, and the next day arrive at Miletus (15). Here he leaves Trophimus sick (2 Tim. iv. 20), and writes his first epistle to Timothy (1 Tim. i. 3). "These things write I unto thee, hoping to come unto thee shortly" (1 Tim. iii. 14); "till I come" (iv. 13). He calls to him there the elders from Ephesus

Writes First to Timothy.

(Acts xx. 17), addressing whom he says, "I know that ye all, among whom I have gone preaching the kingdom of God, shall see my face no more" (ver. 25; see also ver. 38). Thence they sail by Coos, Rhodes, Patara, and Cyprus, landing at Tyre in Phœnicia, and after seven days sail to Ptolemais, and thence to Cæsarea in Palestine, staying with Philip many days. They then pack up their baggage, and go by land to Jerusalem (Acts xxi.).

59. Shortly after his arrival a riot takes place in the Temple enclosure. Paul is taken prisoner by the Roman governor, Claudius Lysias, and sent to Cæsarea (Acts xxiii. 23). *Pentecost, early in the summer.*

60. Felix keeps Paul there two years (xxiv. 27). *Detained.*

61. At his first trial in Cæsarea, when no man stood by him, before Festus, he appeals to Cæsar, the Emperor Nero (xxv. 11). Is heard by King Agrippa, and sent to Rome in the autumn. *Appeals to Cæsar.*

JOURNEY TO ROME.

A.D. 61. Sail from Cæsarea in Palestine, touch at Sidon, sail under Cyprus to Myra of Lycia, where they trans-ship. Then by Cnidus, Cape Salmone of Crete (Candia), to the Fair Havens, the port of Lasea. Here they stayed some time, and Paul left Titus here as bishop of the church (Titus i. 5). *Autumn.*

From Crete they passed the island of Clauda (Gozzo or Ghaudo), and are wrecked on the island of Malta. *October.*

Thence they take ship to Syracuse, hence to Rhegium, from there to Puteoli, where they tarried seven days. By the Consular Way they struck the Via Appia at Capua, and followed that road to Rome, being met at Appii Forum, forty-three miles from Rome, and at Tres Tabernæ, eleven miles from Rome, by the brethren (Acts xxvii. and xxviii.). *After three months.*

62. They arrive in Rome, and Paul is consigned by Julius to the captain of the Prætorian guard— that is, to the officer commanding the guard at the gate of the camp, not to the prefect or general of the Prætorians. *June.*

64. And Paul dwelt two whole years in his own hired house (Acts xxviii. 30).

TIMOTHEUS AND TIMOTHY.

Many minds have been confused by the names Timothy and

Timotheus. They are so confounded in the Bible references that it is of necessity that their individuality should be established.

TIMOTHEUS OF LYSTRA

Is thus spoken of in the Acts (xvi. 1):—"Then came he to Derbe and Lystra: and, behold, a certain disciple was there, named Timotheus, the son of a certain woman, which was a Jewess, and believed; but his father was a Greek."

Of this Timotheus, who was a constant companion of St. Paul, the apostle always speaks as his brother in the faith and fellow-worker (1 Thess. iii. 2; 2 Cor. i. 1, 19, viii. 22; Rom. xvi. 21; Col. i. 1; Heb. xiii. 23; Phil. i. 1, ii. 19; Philemon i. 1).

It was this Timotheus whom Paul sent into Macedonia (Acts xix. 22) with Erastus in A.D. 58, when he was staying at Ephesus till Pentecost.

Paul speaks of him as being with him in Rome as late as A.D. 63 in his epistle to the Philippians (i. 1).

Martyr, January 24, 92.

TIMOTHY OF EPHESUS

This is he whom Paul calls his son in the faith (1 Tim. i. 2, 18; 2 Tim. i. 2), and to whom Paul addressed the two epistles, and whom he sent to the Corinthians (1 Cor. iv. 17, xvi. 10). Paul tells us his grandmother was Lois, and his mother Eunice (2 Tim. i. 5).

He was a young man when Paul sent him to the Corinthians, therefore he says (xvi. 11), "Let no man despise him;" and in writing to Timothy he says, "Let no man despise thy youth" (1 Tim. iv. 12).

It was this Timothy whom Paul sent to the Corinthians with Titus (2 Cor. viii. 6, xii. 18) in A.D. 58, when he was staying at Ephesus till Pentecost.

In 64 Paul writes his last letter to him, and asks him to come to him (2 Tim. iv 9, 21).

Martyr, August 22, 64.

These are only a few of the references, but sufficient to establish the fact. There are many others which confirm the above.

PROPOSED JOURNEYS.

In writing to the Romans (xv. 24) Paul promises to visit Rome on his way to Spain. He says—"Whensoever I take my journey into Spain, I will come to you: for I trust to see you in my journey, and to be brought on my way thitherward by you, if first I be somewhat filled with your company." He then speaks of his last visit to Jerusalem, and adds, "I will come by you into Spain" (28). Because Paul intended to do a thing, it does not follow that he did it; in fact, we know that he often proposed, but that God disposed. Thus—"They assayed to go into Bithynia: but the Spirit suffered them not" (Acts xvi. 7).

So likewise he intended visiting the Corinthians a second time before he did (1 Cor. xvi. 2, 3), and writes most positively of his coming and arrangements—"Now I will come unto you, when I shall pass through Macedonia: for I do pass through Macedonia. And it may be that I will abide, yea, and winter with you, that ye may bring me on my journey whithersoever I go" (ver. 5, 6). He did not make this promised visit, as he explains to them in his second epistle: "I was minded to come unto you before, that ye might have a second benefit; and to pass by you into Macedonia, and to come again out of Macedonia unto you, and of you to be brought on my way toward Judæa" (2 Cor. i. 15). He then explains why he did not go: "When I therefore was thus minded, did I use lightness? or the things that I purpose, do I purpose according to the flesh?" (17.) "Moreover I call God for a record upon my soul, that to spare you I came not as yet unto Corinth" (23). After writing a long letter he winds up by saying, "This is the third time I am coming to you" (xiii. 1). This third time of coming was the second time of going. So he proposed to go to Timothy, but did not (1 Tim. iii. 14). In like manner he proposed visiting Rome before he did: "If by any means now at length I might have a prosperous journey by the will of God to come unto you" (Rom. i. 10). We know how his prayer was answered. He came as a captive, not voluntarily. "Oftentimes I purposed to come unto you, but was let hitherto" (13). Later on Paul, as we all know, came to Rome a prisoner in bonds, and not of his own free will. Here his life was cut short, and so the proposed journey into Spain never took place. So also the supposed visit to Britain falls to the ground.

III.

THE ROAD TO ROME.

TOWARDS the close of a warm summer day in the month of June A.D. 62 the loiterers on the quay at Puteoli noticed a ship entering their bay under full sail. This, to them not unusual custom, denoted that it was a ship of Alexandria, which was soon recognized as an old frequenter of the port, "whose sign was Castor and Pollux" (Acts xxviii. 11). She had wintered at Melita (Malta), and with her passengers and cargo of corn, after touching at Syracuse, went thence to Rhegium; "and after one day the south wind blew, and we came the next day to Puteoli" (Pozzuoli)—ver. 13. On the ship coming up to the quay those on shore would speedily get into conversation with those on board, and it was soon noised abroad that prisoners were amongst the passengers. The Christians of the town claimed St. Paul, and prevailed upon the centurion Julius to rest his prisoners here after their long and perilous journey; as St. Luke says, "Where we found brethren, and were desired to tarry with them seven days: and so we went toward Rome" (Acts xxviii. 14).

Puteoli.

Remains of the quay on which St. Paul landed may still be seen at Pozzuoli, as Puteoli is now called, and of which we give an engraving. Many other Roman remains exist here which in St. Paul's time stood in all their splendour, but we cannot say if they were visited by him. His time would doubtless be given to the Christians of the town, whom he would strengthen and confirm in the faith.

Too soon the week passed away, and then commenced the long march to Rome, one hundred and seventy miles distant, leaving Puteoli by the Consular Way (Via Consularis) to Capua, where they struck into the Via Appia, one hundred and fifty-one miles from Rome. Resting here one night, they proceeded along the "queen of long roads," and by easy stages toward Rome. From the time

Journey to Rome.

Via Appia.

ST. PAUL'S LANDING-PLACE AT PUTEOLI.

of leaving the coast till their arrival in the Eternal City only two small places are mentioned, but, of course, many of interest were passed. Two days after leaving Capua they would arrive at Terracina, seventy-five miles from Rome; and next morning, continuing their way, in two and a half miles they would cross the stream which flows from the Fountain of Feronia.

Grove of Feronia.

"And where Feronia's grove and temple stand."—VIRGIL, Æn., viii. 800.

Servius tells us that "this goddess delighted in freedom, and took deserving slaves under her protection; and they received their liberty by being seated on a chair in her temple, on which was inscribed—'Let slaves who have conducted themselves well sit down here and rise up free.'" Mentioned by Tacitus, "H.," iii. 76. It is supposed to have been founded by a colony of Lacedæmonians (Dionysius, ii. 49).

The Grove of Feronia was on the edge of the Pontine Marshes, and in St. Paul's day no road existed through them, the road being made afterwards by Trajan

The Pontine Marshes.

in his third consulship, as recorded by Dion Cassius and in the inscriptions at Terracina and Tre Ponte, by the relief on the Arch of Constantine, and by a coin of Trajan's. Traffic was conducted through the marshes by means of a canal, which still exists; and passengers coming to Rome embarked at the Grove of Feronia, and were towed in barges through the marshes—

"Where the wet road the Pontine Marsh divides."—LUCIAN, lii. 85.

"The water here was of so foul a stream....
The fenny frogs with croakings hoarse and deep,
And gnats loud buzzing."—HORACE, Sat., i. 6.

"Near to Terracina, advancing in the direction of Rome, a canal runs through the Pontine Marshes, instead of the Via Appia. It is supplied at intervals by water from the rivers. Travellers generally sail up it by night, embarking in the evening, and landing in the morning to travel the rest of their journey by the road. However, during the day the passage-boat is towed by mules" (Strabo, v. 3, 6). Procopius ("De Bel. Got.," i. 19) calls the canal *Decanovius*, and speaks of the Goths having encamped on it at Regeta, thirty-five miles from Rome, when they elected Vitiges their king in 536.

After a long, slow journey St. Paul and his companions landed at Appii Forum, forty-three miles from the imperial city. From hence the march would be resumed in company with many fellow-Christians who had come from Rome to lighten the apostle's way with their fellowship. Appii Forum was a town of the Volsci, and named the Forum of Appius from Appius Claudius, who founded here a market for the convenience of the country people when he made the Appian Way, B.C. 312. It is mentioned by Pliny (iii. 9) in his list of colonies.

Appii Forum.

About one hundred years before this journey of St. Paul another celebrated man passed over the same ground on his way from Rome, through Capua, to Brundusium. Horace accompanied Mæcenas and Virgil in their journey to reconcile Augustus and Antony, and has left us an interesting account of his trip. He divided the distance between Rome and Appii Forum into two stages, saying that fast travellers only did it in one: and the caravan with St. Paul did the same—Horace breaking the journey at Ariccia, sixteen miles from Rome; Paul at the last halting-place, Tres Tabernæ, eleven Roman miles from the city of his captivity. Horace left Appii Forum in the evening, and reached Feronia at

Horace's journey.

ten A.M., doing the distance of the canal (nineteen miles) in fourteen hours.

"At ten, Feronia, we thy fountain gain;
Then land and bathe."—Sat., i. 5.

Suetonius ("Tiberius," ii.) says : "Claudius Drusus erected a statue of himself, wearing a crown, at Appii Forum." Cicero mentions it, and writes from hence, B.C. 59, one of his letters (ii. 10) to Atticus. Horace describes it as "stuffed with sailors and surly landlords." Some fragments of ruins and the forty-third milestone are all that remain of Appii Forum. No doubt St. Paul was as glad as Horace was to leave this part of his journey behind him, and to proceed, with his companions and friends from Rome, upon his journey. They would soon pass beneath the walls of Lanuvium, founded by Æneas, and the birth-place of P. Sulpicius Quirinus, who is mentioned by St. Luke (ch. ii. 2) as Cyrenius, the governor of Syria when the Emperor Augustus made a decree that all the world should be taxed. The slope of *Cyrenius.* the Alban Hills would then be ascended, and from above the Vale of Ariccia the apostle would get his first glimpse of Imperial Rome, far away in the Campagna beyond, *Ariccia.* its buildings glistening in the summer sun. Descending the fine causeway of the Via Appia, the massive ruins of which still excite our admiration, and passing by the tomb of Aruns, the son of Lars Porsena of Clusium, and by the *Tomb of Aruns.* villa of Pompey, which afterwards belonged to Domitian, now the town of Albano, the company would enter what might be called a street of tombs. From this point a long straight road led up to the Porta Capena, and on either side of the way were tombs, the monuments of Rome's great men ; whilst at the end of all, the tombs of the dead expanded, as it were, into a city of the living. On the descent of the hills the apostle might well stop at the still existing tomb of Pompey to take in his last *Tomb of Pompey.* view of the sea, his connecting link between the past and the future, and to gaze upon the splendid city spread before him. At the thirteenth mile he would pass the villa, Sta. Caterina, which was public property ; at eleven and a half miles the tomb of Clodius ; and, on his left, Bovillæ. "Coriolanus took Bovillæ, which is little more than eleven miles from Rome" (Plutarch). "A chapel was consecrated to the Julian family, and statues to the deified Augustus at Bovillæ" (Tacitus, "A.," ii. 41). Beyond, on his left, the road from Antium to Tusculum crosses the Appian Way. Here the caravan would halt for the night at Tres Tabernæ, eleven Roman miles from their destination. Here St. Paul was strengthened by more of the Christians who came to meet him from Rome. "And from thence, when the brethren heard of us, they came to meet us as far as Appii forum, and The three taverns: whom when Paul saw, he thanked God, and took courage" (Acts xxviii. 15).

Tres Tabernæ.

Tres Tabernæ was the first *mansio* or *mutatio*—that is, halting-place for relays—from Rome, or the last on the way to the city. At this point three roads run into the Via Appia—that from Tusculum, that from Alba Longa, and that from Antium; so necessarily here would be a halting-place, which took its name from the three shops there—the general store, the blacksmith's, and the refreshment-house. Cicero tells us ("Ad Atticum," ii. 10, 12) that it took him six hours to do the distance (thirty-two miles) between Tres Tabernæ and Appii Forum. Tres Tabernæ is translated in our Bible as the Three Taverns, but it more correctly means three shops. The site is well identified, not only by tradition, but by classical authority. (See page 70.)

Cicero, writing to Atticus on the 12th of April 58 B.C. from the Three Taverns, gives some important points as to its site. He had come up from his villa at Antium, on his way to Formiæ. "Leaving Antium," he says, "I had just gone from the Antian into the Appian Way at the Tres Tabernæ, during the festival of Ceres, when my friend Curio, coming from Rome, met me. At the same place presently came the servant from you with letters" ("Ad Atticum," ii. 12). In a following letter from Appii Forum, Cicero speaks of having written to Atticus from the Three Taverns; and also in a later letter, for it appears Atticus did not receive the first one (ii. 10, 13).

Letters of Cicero.

Cicero had left his villa at Antium, and the road from thence runs into the Via Appia at the eleventh mile from Rome, as we have seen, so that Tres Tabernæ would be the first halting-place on the Appian Way for Cicero, where he could and did write to Atticus whilst the horses were being changed.

Here, at the farm of Titus Sextus Gallius, now of the Colonnas, was the shrine of the Bona Dea, where Clodius was wounded, and then carried into the neighbouring tavern, where he was murdered (Cicero, "Pro Milo."). The place is now called Frattocchie, and a tavern still exists there. It is exactly 9 English miles 326 yards 2 feet from the Porta Appia, the present Porta S. Sebastiano. It is where the Via Appia Nova joins the Via Appia, eleven miles from the Porta S. Giovanni.

St. Paul and his companions would no doubt make an early start from the Three Taverns, so as to arrive in Rome before the heat of the day. Many monuments still exist which they would pass. At the ninth mile from the Porta Capena, on his left, we now see the ruined tomb of Gallienus, which was used afterwards for the Cæsar Flavius Valerius Severus. He was murdered at the state villa, thirteen miles from Rome, beyond the Three Taverns, and his body was brought back to the tomb of Gallienus, A.D. 307, "which is nine miles from the city on the Appian Way, near the Three Taverns" (Aurelius Victor, "Ep.," xl. 43). The tomb consists of two stories of brickwork, with niches for statues on the outside. It is circular, and of considerable size. Behind are some ruined walls, remains of the villa of Gallienus, where the Discobolus by Naukides, now in the Vatican, was found. Half a mile further on, on his right, Paul would pass the beautiful brick tomb of Quintus Verannius, who was consul A.D. 49, and died in Britain in 55. The next object of interest would be on his left—the Temple of Hercules, standing in the area of Silvanus. This temple was founded in the time of the Republic, and was therefore standing in St. Paul's day. It was shortly after restored by Domitian, and the face of the god was the likeness of the emperor. Martial mentions it, and gives the distance both from Rome and from Alba, with which record the remains agree:— *Tomb of Gallienus and Severus.* *Temple of Hercules.*

"Cæsar, having deigned to assume the form of the mighty Hercules, adds a new temple to the Appian Way, at the spot where the traveller who visits the grove of Diana (at Ariccia) reads the inscription on the eighth milestone from the queen of cities" (ix. 64).

"O Appian Way, which Cæsar consecrates under the form of Hercules, and renders the most celebrated of Italian roads......listen now to the deeds of the greater Hercules, whom the sixth milestone from the citadel of Alba celebrates" (ix. 101).

Domitian had a villa where Albano now stands. This is what Martial refers to, not Alba Longa. In Prince Torlonia's Museum there is a statue of Domitian as Hercules.

In the following, Martial gives some particulars of the route: "Yonder, Faustinus, where the Capenian Gate drips with large drops, and where the Almo cleanses the Phrygian sacrificial knives of the mother of the gods, where the sacred meadow of the Horatii lies verdant, and where the little temple of Hercules swarms with many a visitor" (iii. 47).

IMPERO
DOMIN . SILVANI
C COSSVTIVS . C . LIB . EPAPHRODITVS
ARAM . SILVANO . MARMORAVIT . ITEM
SIMVLACRVM . HERCVLIS . RESTITVIT . ITEM
AEDICULAM . ET . ARAM . EIVSDEM . CORRVPTA
REF . DEDICAVIT . K . MARTIS
P . CALVISIO . RVSONE . L . CAESENNIO
PAETO.

From the above inscription, now in the Capitoline Museum, we learn that the temple was restored by Caius Cossutius, a freedman of Epaphroditus, Nero's secretary, in March 61—that is, the year before Paul passed by it. From the remains, the size and shape of the temple can be distinctly traced. It was square, and the columns were of Alban stone, the walls being of *opus reticulatum*, formed with blocks of silex stone. It stands in an open space on the left of the road, near a round Republican tomb, and a brick one of the first century. The open space was the area of Silvanus. In the field was the villa of Bassus (Martial, iii. 47).

Descending the hill, on the right was the villa of Persius, the Roman satirical poet, and his beautiful brick tomb. "He died on the eighth before the kalends of December (November 24, 62), in the consulship of Rubrius Marius and Asinius Gallus. He ended his days at his villa near the eighth mile on the Appian Way" (Suetonius).

The seventh milestone is on the balustrade of the Capitol. At the half-mile is the scene of the celebrated battle between the three Roman and three Latin champions, the Horatii and the Curiatii,
Tomb of the Horatii. which is marked by the tomb of the two Horatii, surmounted by a medieval tower, called Tor di Selce.
"The Romans buried in a splendid manner the Horatii who were slain, in the place where they fell" (Dionysius, iii. 22).

At the sixth mile is the massive round tomb of Cotta, now called Castel Rotondo, because used as a fortress in the middle ages. It is the tomb of Messella Corvinus, the historian and poet, who died in
Tomb of Cotta. A.D. 11, and was erected to him by Marcus Aurelius Messallinus Cotta, who was consul in A.D. 20, and the tomb was in the height of its beauty as the apostle passed by it.

TOMB OF CECILIA METELLA.

Beyond, at the fifth mile, are the tombs of the three Curiatii.

Tombs of the Curiatii.
Livy (i. 25) says the sepulchres existed in his day, and we can still see how exactly they answer his description: "The sepulchres still remain in the several spots where the combatants fell: those of the two Romans in one place near to Alba; those of the three Albans on the side next to Rome, but in different places, as they fought."

On the right is the tomb of Pomponius Atticus, the friend of Nepos and of Cicero. "He was buried by the Appian Way, near the fifth mile from the city, B.C. 33, February 28" (Cornelius Nepos).

CLAUDIAN AQUEDUCT.

At the fourth mile they passed by the village Pagus Lemonius and the villa of Seneca, in which he was murdered.

Villa of Seneca.
"Seneca had that very day, either from chance or design, returned from Campania, and rested at a villa of his, four miles from Rome" (Tacitus, "Ann.," xv. 60). His tomb, erected shortly after this date (65), is still standing; also the walls of the Temple of Jupiter, belonging to the village, and away to the right the then newly-erected Claudian aqueduct (50). There is no authority for any meeting or communication between St. Paul and Seneca; but Paul was once brought before his brother's tribunal in A.D. 53, when

Gallio.
Gallio was proconsul of Achaia, as recorded in Acts xviii. 12. At the third mile they would pass the

Tomb of Cecilia Metella.
well-known tomb of Cecilia Metella, the wife of

ARCH OF DRUSUS.

Lucius Cornelius Sylla, the dictator; and at the first mile, through the comparatively newly-erected Arch of Drusus, brother of Tiberius, and father of Germanicus, decreed 8 B.C.

Arch of Drusus.

"The senate likewise, among various other honours, decreed for him a triumphal arch of marble, with trophies, in the Appian Way, and gave the cognomen of Germanicus to him and his posterity" (Suetonius, "Claudius," i.).

Just beyond, on the right, are the columbaria of the servants of the imperial family, in an almost perfect state, but discovered some years ago. They lie upon the right of the pathway, and possess considerable interest, not only as good specimens of the chambers where the ashes of those who were cremated were deposited, but special interest is attached to some of the names found therein—names that are mentioned in the New Testament. The question arises, Are these the remains of those there mentioned? can we still look upon the ashes of those early Christians? Let us see.

Columbaria of Cæsar's household.

In the first columbaria we find this inscription on the end wall to the left, at the bottom of the stairs: AMPLIATVS-RESTITVTO.FRATR-SVO. FECIT.MERENTI. On the next wall is: D. M.-TRYPHAENAE-VALERIA. TRYPHAENA-MATRI. B. M. F. ET-VALERIVS-FUTIANUS. (Tryphænæ Valeria and Valerius Futianus to the memory of the mother Tryphæna.) Just beyond is: DOMITIAE.L. FAUSTILLAE-PETRONIO. ARISTONIS.L.-EPAPHRAE. Upon the stair wall is a Greek inscription to a certain Onesimus.

Upon the outside of the second, built into the wall, is: D. M.- VARIA.TRYPHOSA-PATRONA.ET.M. EPPIUS.CLEMENS-CONIUGI.BENE- MERENTI FEC.VARIAE.PRIMAE F.-VIXIT.ANN.XXX.—(Varia Tryphosa, patron, and M. Eppius Clemens erected this to his well-beloved wife, who lived thirty years.)

Close by is: D. M. S.-LIBERTI.LIBER-TAL.C. JULIUS-PHILAETUS- C. JULIUS.PRYPHO)-C. JULIUS.ONESI-MUS.TULIA.EUTHI-CIA.JULIA- HELPIS-JULIA.CLAPHURA-FECERUNT.

Inside the second, *in situ*, is the inscription: ONESIMUS.A.PORTICU.

These two cases of the name Onesimus are simply a coincidence, as they do not refer to St. Paul's convert, he having been sent back to his master. This name was common, and occurs on other slabs.

These columbaria were for the servants or officers of the imperial family, and date from Cæsar to Nero, both inclusive. The historic notices of some of these names are valuable.

St. Paul, writing to the Romans from Corinth, A.D. 58, says

(xvi. 12), "Salute Tryphena and Tryphosa, who labour in the Lord." Writing from Rome to the Colossians, A.D. 62, he says (iv. 9), "With Onesimus, a faithful and beloved brother;" and to Philemon (ver. 10), "I beseech thee for my son Onesimus, whom I have begotten in my bonds." In Colossians i. 7 we have, "As ye also learned of Epaphras our dear fellowservant;" and in ch. iv. 12, "Epaphras, who is one of you, a servant of Christ;" who is again mentioned in Philemon 23: "There salute thee Epaphras, my fellowprisoner in Christ Jesus." "Salute Ampliatus, my beloved in the Lord", (Rom. xvi. 8).

Now, these names are uncommon, with the above exception, and we have them mentioned only by St. Paul and on these marble slabs, which slabs are in the columbaria of the freedmen of the Cæsars, agreeing in date with the time of St. Paul's letters, who himself preached to and had converts amongst the household of Cæsar, in the Prætorian Camp, and in the Imperial Palace upon the Palatine Hill. He says, writing to the Philippians (ch. i. 13), "So that my bonds in Christ are manifest in all the prætorium [camp], and in all other places;" and in ch. iv. 22, "All the saints salute you, chiefly they that are of Cæsar's household."

The name Valeria was taken, when she obtained her freedom, from her mistress, the Empress Messalina (whose name was Valeria). These names do not cover their own ashes, but are memorial stones erected to fellow-servants, who, if we may judge from the "D. M." over the inscriptions, were not Christians. They record a work of charity and love to fellow-servants, though not co-religionists, and the names mentioned may well be those likewise named by St. Paul.

The names Ampliatus, Tryphena, and Tryphosa occur before the coming of Paul to Rome, and these, with some others mentioned by him (Rom. xvi.), were found on slabs in another columbaria, about a mile further back, on the Via Appia, discovered in 1726, and known as the columbaria of the servants of Livia Augusta. It is now a complete ruin; one wall only remains: D. M.-FVLVIAE. TRYPHAENAE- C. POMPEIVS. APOLLONIVS-MATRI. OPTIMAE (Gruter, page 729, No. 10). D. M.-C. POMPEIO. APOLLONIO-C. POMPEIVS. APOLLINARIS. F. ET- FVLVIA. TRYPHAENA. CONIVNX-FECERVNT (Gruter, page 737, No. 3). These are the names probably of some members of the church whom Paul greets in writing to Rome, but who are not mentioned again by him after his arrival in the city.

Proceeding on their journey, St. Paul and his companions, passing by the tomb of the Scipios, would soon *The Scipios' tomb.*

cross the stream of the Almo, and enter Rome by the Porta Capena. This gate was in the line of the Servian Wall, between the Cœlian and Aventine Hills, and was excavated by Mr. J. H. Parker in 1867. He found part of one of the towers standing—the channel of the Aqua Appia, which went over the gate and the pavement of the roadway. This gateway is represented on the Arch of Constantine, on two of the reliefs taken from Trajan's Arch. The left hand relief represents Rome receiving the emperor at the Porta Capena, which is shown in the background of the relief with the Temple of Mars, which stood outside that gate. The other relief shows the same gate, and records the fact that Trajan was the first who made the Appian Road to pass through the Pontine Marshes. Before his time the journey across the marshes was made by the canal. The Porta Capena is shown in the background; whilst the emperor is standing over a female figure, who represents the Via Appia, and the wheel on which she is reclining is symbolic of locomotion.

The Almo.

Porta Capena.

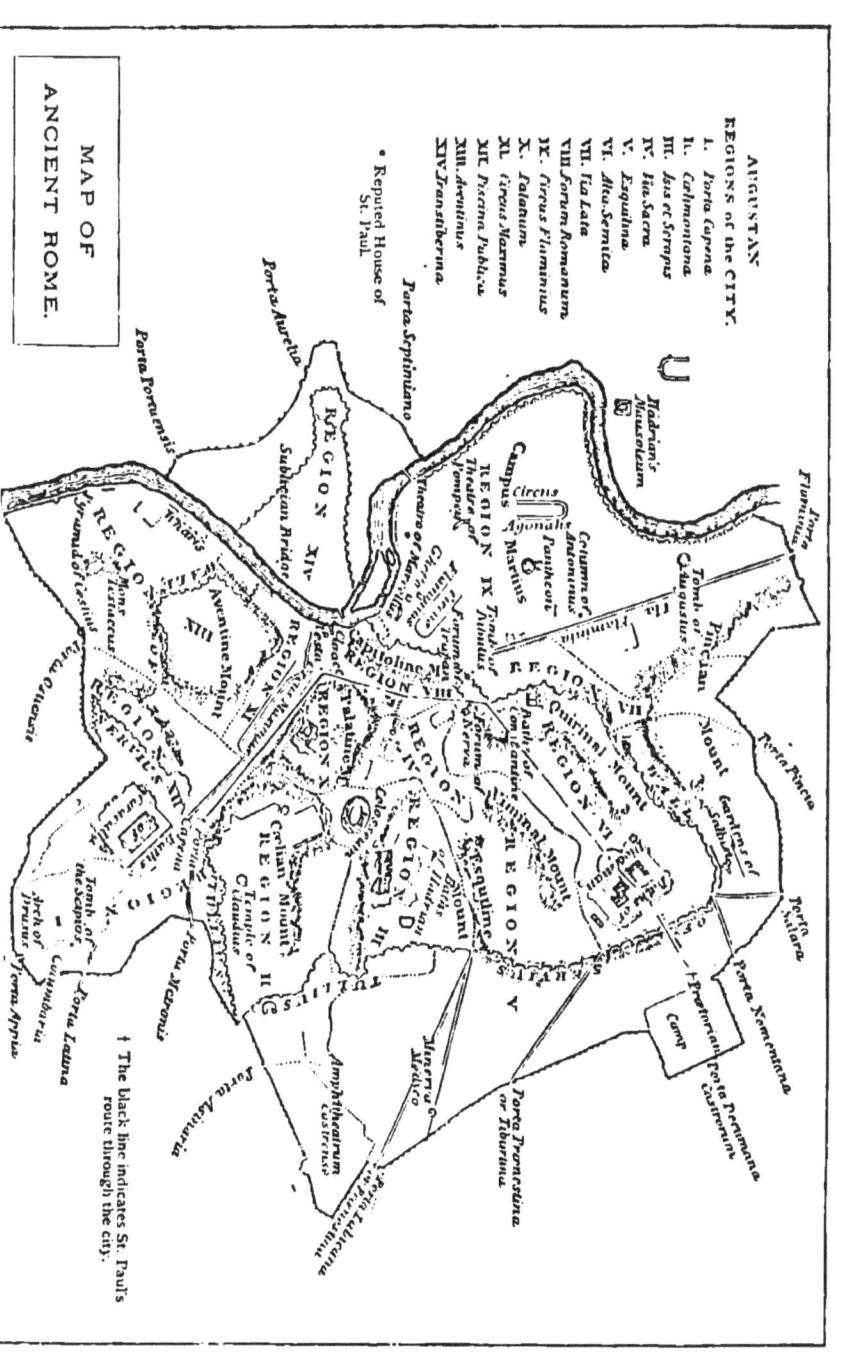

IV.

ROMANUS SUM.

Route through city.
ARRIVING at the city gate, St. Paul's route would be across the city to the Prætorian Camp, situated on the neck of the Viminal Hill. We cannot say positively which way they went, but, considering that the direct way now, by the Colosseum, was then barred by the house and gardens of Nero, the probability is that they passed along the street by the side of the Circus Maximus, Vicus Malians, then along the Vicus Tuscus, under the Palatine, through the Forum Romanum, and thence by the Argiletum (Via Bonella), through the Forum of Augustus, and along the Vicus Longus (Via Nazionale), to the Prætorian Camp. There Julius handed over his charge to the captain of the guard at the gate of the camp.

Prætorian Camp.

"And when we came to Rome, the centurion delivered the prisoners to the captain of the guard: but Paul was suffered to dwell by himself with a soldier that kept him" (Acts xxviii. 16). This privilege was accorded to him because he was a Roman, for it was against the law to put a Roman into prison without trial. We have many instances of this in Roman history: and "so Junius Gallio, brother of Seneca, was kept under a guard in the house of a magistrate" (Tacitus, "Annals," vi. 3).

Paul himself frequently asserted that he was a Roman citizen, and made use of this privilege several times when in difficulties; at the same time, he boasted of being a Jew and a Pharisee.

Paul a Jew.
"Paul said, I am a man which am a Jew of Tarsus, a city in Cilicia, a citizen of no mean city" (Acts xxi. 39). And again, "I am verily a man which am a Jew, born in Tarsus, a city in Cilicia, yet brought up in this city"—Jerusalem—(ch. xxii. 3). In writing to the Corinthians, he says, "Are they Hebrews? so am I. Are they Israelites? so am I. Are they the seed of Abraham? so am I" (2 Cor. xi. 22). And to the Philippians (ch. iii. 5), "Circumcised the eighth day, of the stock of Israel, of the

THE FORUM ROMANUM RESTORED.

tribe of Benjamin, an Hebrew of the Hebrews; as touching the law, a Pharisee." And in Acts xxiii. 6, "I am a Pharisee, the son of a Pharisee." "After the most straitest sect of our religion I lived a Pharisee" (ch. xxvi. 5). Notwithstanding all this, directly he gets into trouble he says he is a Roman, and claims the privileges. When at Philippi, a Roman colony in Macedonia, Paul and Silas were put into prison after having been beaten, *Imprisoned at Philippi.* and when the magistrates sent the next morning to release them, "Paul said unto them, They have beaten us openly uncondemned, being Romans, and have cast us into prison; and now do they thrust us out privily? nay *Paul a Roman.* verily; but let them come themselves and fetch us out. And the serjeants told these words unto the magistrates: and they feared, when they heard that they were Romans" (Acts xvi. 37, 38).

When Claudius Lysias, chief captain of Jerusalem, had rescued Paul from the people, he "bade that he *Apprehended at Jerusalem.* should be examined by scourging......And as they bound him with thongs, Paul said unto the centurion that stood by,

Is it lawful for you to scourge a man that is a Roman, and uncondemned? When the centurion heard that, he went and told the chief captain, saying, Take heed what thou doest: for this man is a Roman. Then the chief captain came, and said unto him, Tell me, art thou a Roman? He said, Yea. And the chief captain answered, With a great sum obtained I this freedom. And Paul said, But I was free born. Then straightway they departed from him which should have examined him: and the chief captain also was afraid, after he knew that he was a Roman, and because he had bound him" (Acts xxii. 24–29).

Sent to Cæsarea. Lysias, writing to Felix when he sent Paul to Cæsarea, says, "Then came I with an army, and rescued him, having understood that he was a Roman" (ch. xxiii. 27).

Before Felix. After his arrival he had several interviews with Felix the governor, who was the brother of Pallas, the favourite of Claudius (Tacitus, "Annals," xii. 54). "But after two years Porcius Festus came into Felix' room: and *Dwells there two years.* Felix, willing to shew the Jews a pleasure, left Paul bound"—A.D. 60—(Acts xxiv. 27). He was shortly *Before Festus.* after brought before Festus, who asked Paul if he was willing to be tried at Jerusalem. "Then said Paul, I stand at Cæsar's judgment seat, where I ought to be judged......I appeal unto Cæsar" (ch. xxv. 10, 11). *Appealeth unto Cæsar.* He was afterwards brought before King Agrippa, who was on a visit to Festus, and after hearing him, *Before Agrippa.* "Agrippa said unto Festus, This man might have been set at liberty, if he had not appealed unto Cæsar" (ch. xxvi. 32).

From all this we see that St. Paul was a Roman, and free-born. The question naturally arises, How could he be a Jew *How a Jew and a Roman.* and a Roman? It was the custom of the Roman senate under the empire to give the privileges of citizenship to any who had done some favour for Rome, and at the same time many bought this privilege. But under the republic, *Tarsus.* colonies and cities had this privilege bestowed upon them. Tarsus, in Cilicia, was an important city, and celebrated for its school of literature and philosophy. During the civil wars it had opened its gates to Cæsar and Mark Antony, who bestowed special favours upon it. Dion Cassius (x. 57) says, "It sided with Julius Cæsar in the civil war, and afterwards with Augustus; and from Cæsar it was named Juliopolis, and honoured with the greatest privileges." Whether the honour of Roman citizens was then bestowed upon its inhabitants, amongst others Paul's father, we cannot say. Tarsus was a Roman colony, and it is designated on a coin of Augustus as Libera Civitas. We were taught at school that from an inscription it was known that for a supply of corn sent to Rome during a scarcity this privilege was bestowed. However that may be, Paul's father was free, and so his son was free-born. It may have happened in this way. Saulus the elder was at some time a slave of Paulus Æmilius, *Of the Æmilian gens.* and on obtaining his freedom, either by gift or by purchase, took the cognomen of Paulus from his former master—a usual custom; hence his son, the apostle, was called Saulus Paulus. In those days a man was generally known by his prænomen or Christian name. We have the apostle introduced to us as Saul, and he is so called some time after his conversion; but after he was chosen to preach to the Gentiles, and during his mission to Cyprus after his interview with the governor Sergius Paulus (Acts xiii. 7), he is spoken of as "Saul, who is also *Sergius Paulus.* called Paul." He could not use the Roman name Paulus without permission of the head of the *gens;* and so he went to Cyprus, and having obtained that privilege is re-introduced to us as Paul.

Behind the Church of S. Biagio della Pagnotta, on the Via Giulia, and thirteen yards from the river, the following interesting cippus or boundary stone of Claudius came to light in the month of August 1887 (now preserved in the east cloister of the National Museum at the Baths of Diocletian) :—

PAVLLVS . FABIVS . PERSi*cus*	*He was Consul A.D. 34.*
C . EGGIVS . MARVLL*us* .	
L . SERGIVS . PAVLLVS .	*Proconsul of Cyprus A.D. 45.*
C . OBELLIVS . RV*fus*	
L . SCRIBONIV*s* . *Libo*	
CVRATORE*s riparum*	
ET . ALV*ei Tiberis*	
EX . AVCTORIT*ate*	
TI . CLAVDI . CAESARIS	
AVG . GERMANICI	
PRINCIPIS . *Censor*	*A D. 47.*
RIPAM . CIPPIS . POS*itis*	
TERMINAVERVNT . A . TR*ig* AR*io*	
AD . PONTEM . AGRIPPAE	

The Emperor Claudius assumed the censorship A.D. 47 (Suetonius, "Claudius," xvi.). In A.D. 15 Tiberius appointed five conservators of senatorial rank to regulate the water in the river (Dion Cassius, lvii. 14). Of course this included keeping the banks in repair, and other hydraulic matters. From the above inscription the commission must have been continued; for it records the names of five curators of the banks and channel of the Tiber under the authority of Claudius A.D. 47, and records the bounds laid down from the Trigarium, the chariot drive (Pliny, xxxvii. 77), to the bridge of Agrippa, just above the Ponte Sisto.

Greater interest, however, attaches to this inscription from another historical point of view. The third name mentioned is that of Lucius Sergius Paullus, at that time head of the great Æmilian gens. This is the same Sergius Paulus mentioned in St. Luke's narrative of the Acts of the Apostles (ch. xiii.), who was proconsul of Cyprus when St. Paul visited the island on his first missionary journey, A.D. 45. In the Acts, Sergius Paulus is described as "a prudent man," who "desired to hear the word of God," before whom Elymas was struck blind by Paul "for seeking to turn away the proconsul from the faith." "Then the proconsul, when he saw what was done, believed, being astonished at the doctrine of the Lord." We have here the important statement that Sergius Paulus became a Christian. He was the head of the *gens* with which Paul's father was connected; hence Saul had claims on him, and in their interviews he evidently granted to Saul the privilege of using the name Paulus—"Saul, who is likewise called Paul." Paul's mother was probably of this *gens*, who, when her Jewish husband died, married the Roman Pudens, and lived in Rome; for Paul in A.D. 58, in writing to the Romans, salutes her and his half-brother Rufus Pudens (Rom. xvi. 13). After serving his three years, Sergius Paulus returned to Rome, and, we now find, was appointed a Tiber commissioner under Claudius in A.D. 47. The only other record we have of this Christian governor, and that but just discovered, is another confirmation of the truth of the Bible history. Sergius Paulus probably died before the writing of the Epistle to the Romans, for he is not saluted in it.

In 1879 an interesting monument, erected by St. Paul's fellow-citizens to Gordianus III., was found on the Sacra Via. A beautiful piece of frieze, inscribed TAPCCωN was supported by columns of porta santa marble. This sustained a canopy, beneath which was the statuette of Gordianus, standing on a pedestal bearing in Greek an inscription, unfortunately much mutilated, which reads: THE IN-

HABITANTS OF TARSUS—WORSHIP TO THE SEVERE GOD—THE AUTOCRAT CÆSAR M. ANTONINUS, SON OF GORDIANUS—RESPECT, HAPPINESS, WORSHIP—LORD OF THE [WHOLE] UNIVERSE—GORDIANA, SEVERIANA, ADRIANA—ANTONINIANA, ADRIANA—THE GREATEST AS WELL AS THE MOST BEAUTIFUL—OF THE PROVINCES—OF CILICIA, ISAURIA, AND LYKAONIA.

It is of importance as showing that at that late period—A.D. 238-241—the connection between Rome and Tarsus was still kept up.

St. Paul, because he was a Roman, was allowed to live in his own hired house till called upon to plead. They could not put him in prison unheard, and as probably he could not find a surety, a soldier was answerable for him. We know from Cicero (against Verres) that it was "a crime to scourge a Roman, a sin to put him in prison uncondemned, and fratricide to put him to death." (See Livy, "Ep." lxi.) *Surveillance.*

Living in his own house, he was allowed to do pretty much as he liked, as formerly at Cæsarea, but not to go beyond the city bounds; and probably he had to present himself at stated times to the authorities. And so "Paul called the chief of the Jews together" (Acts xxviii. 17), and "many came to him into his lodging" (ver. 23). "And Paul dwelt two whole years in his own hired house, and received all that came in unto him, preaching the kingdom of God, and teaching those things which concern the Lord Jesus Christ, with all confidence, no man forbidding him" (ver. 30, 31). *Two years in Rome.*

On the borders of the modern Ghetto there is a house which Jewish tradition has handed down as being the hired house of St. Paul whilst in Rome. The house is of ancient Roman construction, like many others in this part of the city, and the Jewish tradition may be a faithful one. We know that St. Paul was a Jew, and had kinsmen amongst the Jews in Rome, and it is natural to suppose that he would dwell near them. The Ghetto has been a Jewish quarter from the time of Pompey the Great to this day, and doubtless Paul dwelt somewhere there. *St. Paul's house.*

There were several quarters where the Jews had settled in the imperial city—in Trastevere, in the Suburra, on the Esquiline, and in the district of the Æsculetum, by the Tiber. In this latter district Jewish and Roman Catholic traditions meet, as it were, on common ground in their associations about St. Paul. Jewish tradition points to a house at the corner of the Via di S. Bartolomeo dei Vaccinari and the Via degli Strengari, on the left side of this latter street, as the dwelling where he called the chief of the Jews together and explained the gospel to them. The Roman church of S. Paola alla Regola, within one hundred yards of the reputed house, claims that there St. Paul had a school, and they show a chapel attached to the church as the actual school-room. An old work, "Tessori Nascosti dell' Alma Citta di Roma," speaks of the "Divi Pauli Apostoli Hospitium et Schola," in reference to his conversion, Jan. 25th, and says, "Those he converted to Christ came here to be catechised, because it was a retired site." Thus we have two antagonistic faiths meeting on common ground in their testimony about St. Paul, so we may in all probability look upon this as the neighbourhood, if not the actual site, of his dwelling, where "he received all that went in unto him."

The attention of Anglo-Saxon visitors has long been called to this house; and we have repeatedly demonstrated that the long, narrow line of streets, which, under different titles, led along the left bank of the Tiber from the Pons Fabricius to the Pons Triumphalis, was an ancient Roman thoroughfare, and our views have lately received a most striking confirmation.

In the month of August 1888, on the Via Arenula, the new street leading to the new Ponte Garibaldi, at the corner of the Via di S. Bartolomeo dei Vaccinari, the last street on the right which leads up to the reputed house and school of St. Paul, at the depth of twenty-seven feet (which shows how the soil has accumulated) another of the Lares Compilates of the time of Augustus was discovered. It is a square marble altar with a beautiful cornice, which was, unfortunately, broken. On the front is a relief representing four men at a sacrifice, with bay crowns upon their veiled heads. A bull and a pig are by assistants being led up to sacrifice—the bull to the Genius Cæsarum, and the pig to the Lares. On each side of the altar is the figure of a youth, the titular deities, and at the back a crown.

Above the relief in front is the inscription—

LARIBVS . AVGVSTIS
CIVS . C . M
MANIVS C . l . iuSTVS
MAG . VICI . ANNI . NONI

It was dedicated to the Lares of Augustus by four officials of a street nine years after Augustus had restored the street shrines. That was in 6 B.C. (Dion Cassius, lv. 8), so this altar was erected in A.D. 3.

On the right side under the cornice is inscribed—

P . CLODIVS . P

and on the left side—

S . L . L . SALVIVS .

evidently the names of two of the officials.

The altar stands on a travertine base, on which is written—

maGISTRI . VICI . AESCLETI . ANNI . VIIII

which is valuable as giving us the name of the street Vicus Æscletus (Beech Street).

> "Nec rigida mollior æsculo."—HORACE, *Odes*, iii. 10.

> "Altior ac penitus terræ defigitur arbos,
> Æsculus in primis."—VIRGIL, *Georgics*, II. 290.

This is the first mention we have of this street. The victors of the Pythian games were crowned with a chaplet made of beech leaves before the bay (laurel) was used; hence Ovid—

> "Æsculeæ capiebat frondis honorem."—*Met.* i. 449.

Suetonius ("Augustus," xxx.) says, "He divided the city into regions and streets, ordaining that the annual magistrates should take by lot the charge of the former, and that the latter should be superintended by wardens chosen out of the people of each neighbourhood." Pliny ("N. H.," iii. 9) says, "The city is divided into fourteen regions, with two hundred and sixty-five cross streets under the guardianship of the Lares."

The pedestal of the Apollo, leader of the Muses (No. 516), in the Vatican Museum, is an altar dedicated to the Laribus Augustis, Genius Cæsarum, by four street officials; on the left of which is the Genius of Augustus, similar to the statue (555) in the Sala Rotonda.

If the Jewish tradition is correct, that the house of St. Paul was at the angle of the Via S. Bartolomeo dei Vaccinari and the Via degli Strengari, and if the Romish Church tradition is true, that he had a school (room shown) at the Church of S. Paola alla Regola, on the Via S. Paola alla Regola, a continuation of the Via S. Bartolomeo dei Vaccinari, then we have at last arrived at the name of the street where the apostle dwelt for two whole years in his own hired house, 62 to 64—namely, the Vicus Æscletus, probably so called because it led to a grove of beech trees, Æsculus being corrupted into Æscletus.

Pliny (xvi. 15) speaks of this grove: "Q. Hortensius, the dictator, on the secession of the plebeians to the Janiculum (A.U.C. 466), passed a law in the Æsculetum, that what the plebeians had enacted should be binding on every Roman citizen."

The altar has been placed in the centre of the first room of mosaics in the Capitoline Museum, and gives us the name of the street in which Jewish and Roman tradition assigns the memorials of St. Paul, his house and his school.

There is no contemporary or early record in black and white to prove it, but the circumstantial evidence is strong in locating St. Paul in this neighbourhood. The lower part of the house is of ancient construction; it was entered from the street now called Via S. Bartolomeo dei Vaccinari.

Whilst a prisoner at Cæsarea, during the same space of time, the same privilege was granted him: 'And he [Felix] commanded a centurion to keep Paul, and to let him have liberty, and that he should forbid none of his acquaintance to minister or come unto him" (Acts xxiv. 23). So Paul was at liberty to go about the city of Rome, not indeed chained to but accompanied by a soldier; and when the apostle speaks of "these my chains, these bonds," it is simply a figure of speech used to show that he had not his full liberty.

Not chained.

The delay in hearing Paul's case arose from the absence of the emperor from Rome and no accusers appearing against him. Festus' principal idea of bringing him before Agrippa was that he "might have somewhat to write. For it seemeth to me unreasonable to send a prisoner, and not withal to signify the crimes laid against him" (Acts xxv. 26, 27). And the chief men of the Roman Jews said to Paul, "We neither received letters out of Judæa concerning thee, neither any of the brethren that came shewed or spake any harm of thee" (xxviii. 21).

Absence of Nero.

V.

THE EARLY CHURCH IN ROME.

AS a Roman, St. Paul naturally had a desire to visit Rome, but he intended to have come voluntarily. He says (Acts xix. 21), "I must also see Rome;" and in his Epistle to the Romans he says (ch. i. 10), "Making request, if by any means now at length I might have a prosperous journey by the will of God to come unto you." "So, as much as in me is, I am ready to preach the gospel to you that are at Rome also" (ver. 15); and again (ch. xv. 23), "Having a great desire these many years to come unto you." No doubt, as a Christian missionary, he desired to preach to the Romans and to strengthen the young church there; besides, he had many kinsmen in the city (ch. xvi.). And now he was come, not of his own free will, but as a prisoner under surveillance, as the Lord had told him: "So must thou bear witness also at Rome" (Acts xxiii. 11).   *Intention of visiting.*

We have seen that many of the brethren went out to meet him on his approach to Rome, and we know from his epistle to them that there was already a Christian church there. This church was in all probability founded by Aquila and Priscilla, who lived in Rome in the time of the Emperor Claudius, and who had to leave the city, "because that Claudius had commanded all Jews to depart from Rome" (Acts xvii. 2). "He banished from Rome all the Jews, who were continually making disturbances at the instigation of one Chrestus" (Suetonius, "Claudius," xxv.). They evidently returned after that emperor's death, for Paul says, in writing to the Romans (ch. xvi. 3-5), "Greet Priscilla and Aquila my helpers in Christ Jesus: who have for my life laid down their own necks: unto whom not only I give thanks, but also all the churches of the Gentiles. Likewise greet the church that is in their house." Whether they were still in Rome on Paul's arrival or not we cannot say, but the apostle shortly before his   *House of Aquila.*

death, in writing to Timothy at Ephesus, says, "Salute Prisca and Aquila" (2 Tim. iv. 19).

On a lonely and deserted part of the Aventine Hill there is a church dedicated to these saints—a church said to have been erected over their house, in which the primitive church in Rome assembled. From a neighbouring vineyard access may be had to some vaults under the church, which vaults, formed of *opus reticulatum*—network wedges of tufa stone—were no doubt part of a Roman house of the late republic or early empire; and this may indeed have been the dwelling of St. Paul's two friends.

Remains.

The early Christian church in Rome was mainly composed of Jewish converts, as we gather from St. Paul's epistle to them; and his great desire was to establish their church. He says, "Your faith is spoken of throughout the whole world" (ch. i. 8); and again, "I long to see you, that I may impart unto you some spiritual gift, to the end ye may be established; that is, that I may be comforted together with you by the mutual faith both of you and me. Now I would not have you ignorant, brethren, that oftentimes I purposed to come unto you, (but was let hitherto,) that I might have some fruit among you also, even as among other Gentiles" (ver. 11–13).

Jewish converts.

Besides the church assembling in the house of Aquila, we have record of other assemblies in Rome of early Christians, whom St. Paul also salutes in the last chapter of his Roman epistle. In verse 14 he says, "Salute Asyncritus, Phlegon, Hermas, Patrobas, Hermes, and the brethren which are with them." And in the following: "Salute Philologus, and Julia, Nereus, and his sister, and Olympas, and all the saints which are with them." These names are not Jewish, and no doubt these were Gentile Christians holding separate meetings. The church of Hermes, as we shall see, assembled in the house of Pudens. One of the earliest bishops of Rome was Clement, who is mentioned by St. Paul in his Epistle to the Philippians (ch. iv. 3): "And I intreat thee also, true yokefellow, help those women which laboured with me in the gospel, with Clement also, and with other my fellowlabourers, whose names are in the book of life." It has always been the tradition of the Church that Clement, before his exile from Rome, founded a church in his house; and at the peace of the Church a church was founded in connection with his house, which was in the valley between the Cœlian and Esquiline Hills. Thus Jerome

Other churches.

Gentile converts.

The Oratory of St. Clement.

says: "The church built to St. Clement keeps the memory of his name to this day." This church and the house containing the original oratory were destroyed in 1084; and the ruins being filled in, another church was erected on the same site. These facts were brought to light by the late Rev. Father Mullooney, who found below the present church the earlier church of the fourth century, and below that the house and oratory of Clement. Nearly the whole of it has been cleared out, and can now be visited, forming one of the most interesting sights of ancient Rome. *House of Clement.* In the second church several beautiful frescoes were found, one of which represents St. Clement celebrating the Lord's Supper in the chapel which he founded in his house: this was painted about 1050, just before the church was destroyed.

From the salutations of St. Paul we gather that there were many Christians in Rome when he wrote his Epistle to the Romans; and from the salutations contained in the letters from Rome we know that through him the church was considerably augmented and established; and, as we shall see, two churches still exist, both brought to light through the researches of Britons, which date before the end of the first century, and were established during St. Paul's captivity. We allude to the church of Pudens, brought to notice by the late Mr. J. H. Parker of Oxford; and to the oratory in the house of Clement, discovered by the late Rev. Father Mullooney, head of the Irish Dominicans in Rome.

The historian Tacitus has handed down the trials of a Roman lady who was a British princess, and although he does not in direct terms call her a Christian—which the pagan authors of the period called a "foreign superstition," and *Pomponia Græcina.* confounded with Judaism—there is no doubt, from his description, to the unbiassed mind, that she was a Christian; and although her husband declared her blameless, she was evidently a living martyr to her faith.

Tacitus ("Annals," xiii. 32) says: "During Nero's second consulship (A.D. 57), Pomponia Græcina, a lady of distinction, and married to Aulus Plautius,—who, upon his return from Britain, entered the city in ovation,—on being charged with embracing a foreign superstition, was consigned to the adjudication of her husband. Plautius assembled her kindred, and in observance of primitive institution, having in their presence held solemn inquisition upon the conduct and character of his wife, adjudged her innocent. She lived to a great age, and in unintermitted sorrow; for since the fate of Julia (the daughter of Drusus), procured by the perfidy of Messalina, she wore for the space of forty years no habit but that of mourning, nor was grief absent from her breast; a conduct which during the reign of Claudius escaped with impunity, and redounded hereafter to her honour."

Suetonius ("Claudius," xxix.) informs us that Claudius put to death the two Julias, daughters of Drusus and Germanicus, without any proof of guilt, and without hearing them in their defence. This was in A.D. 43. Plautius Lateranus, the nephew of Aulus, was put to death by Nero, A.D. 65, and his estates confiscated, which were afterwards given by Constantine to the bishop of Rome; hence the name is handed down in the Lateran.

Tacitus gives us an account of another trial, in which a Roman lady was accused and condemned, in A.D. 67, which bears evidence that she had sought the aid of the churches' prayers in her distress; probably she had herself joined them. He says: "Ostorius Sabinus, the accuser of Soranus, entered the senate, and proceeded to charge him with 'his friendship for Rubellius Plautus; with having administered his proconsulate of Asia with a view to popularity, and with consulting his own private objects rather than the public benefit, encouraging disaffection in the various communities.' These were old affairs; but a charge of recent date involved the daughter in the father's peril: it was, 'that she had distributed sums of money among the magi.' Such was the fact, it must be admitted; but it arose from the filial piety of Servilia (for that was her name), who, out of affection for her parent, and with the simplicity natural to so young a creature, had merely consulted them 'on the safety of the family—whether Nero would be disposed to mercy, and whether the investigation before the senate would issue in anything of a formidable nature.' Accordingly she was summoned before the senate; and the two parties were stationed on opposite sides before the judgment-seat of the consuls—the father, far advanced in years; the daughter, not yet twenty, widowed, and desolate, her husband, Pollio, having been recently banished. And so oppressed was she with the thought of having added to her father's dangers, that she could not even look towards him.

"The accuser then questioned her, 'Whether she had not sold her bridal ornaments, and even the chain off her neck, to raise money for the performance of magic rites?' At first she fell prostrate upon the floor, and continued for a long time bathed in tears and speechless; afterwards embracing the altar and its appendages, she said, 'I have prayed to no malignant deities; I have used no spells; nor did I seek aught by my unhappy prayers than that you, Cæsar, and you, fathers, would preserve this best of fathers unharmed. With this view I gave up my jewels, my raiment, and the ornaments belonging to my station, as I would have given up my blood and life had they required them. To those men, till then unknown to me, it belongs to declare whose ministers they are and what mysteries they use; the prince's name was never uttered by me except among the gods. Yet to all this proceeding of mine, whatever it were, my most unhappy father is a stranger; and if it be a crime, I alone am the delinquent.'

Her prayer.

"Soranus, while she was yet speaking, caught up her words, and cried with earnestness 'that his daughter went not with him to the province; such was her tender age she could not have been acquainted with Plautus. She was not implicated in the charges against her husband. He implored them, that as her only crime was too much piety, they would separate her case from his; but as for himself, he would submit to whatever fate awaited him.' At the same time, he sprang forward to meet his daughter, who flew to meet him; but the consular lictors stepped between and prevented them.

"The witnesses were then heard......

"Soranus and Servilia were indulged with the choice of their mode of death" ("Annals," xvi. 30).

VI.

THE BRITISH ROYAL FAMILY, ST. PAUL, PUDENS, AND MARTIAL.

AFTER a heroic struggle, Caradoc or Caractacus, the British chief or king of Siluria, fell into the hands of the Romans, and with his family, including his daughter Gladys, was brought prisoner to Rome in 52 A.D. We all know of his noble defence, and how he was released by the Emperor Claudius, and dwelt in Rome. His daughter, being adopted by the emperor, took the Roman names Claudia Peregrina Rufus. Before this, Aulus Rufus Pudens Pudentinus held an official position in the southern part of Britain, and possessed an estate in the neighbourhood of Chichester, where an inscription still records the ground he gave for a temple to Neptune and Minerva. His friend Aulus Plautius, the governor of Southern Britain, whose tomb and inscription exist at the Ponte Lucano on the road to Tivoli, had married Gladys, the sister of Caractacus, who, from her knowledge of Greek literature, took the name of Pomponia Græcina, whose trial we have already alluded to ; so that an intimacy sprang up between Pudens and her niece Gladys or Claudia. Martial the poet, who lived in Rome during the years 49 to 86, was a friend of Pudens, and he thus alludes to his absence in Britain (vi. 58) :—

Caractacus.

Pudens.

"Whilst you, Aulus, delight in a near view of the Arcadian bear, and with enduring the climate of Northern skies, oh, how very nearly had I, your friend, been carried off to the waters of the Styx, and seen the dusky clouds of the Elysian plain ! My eyes, weak as they were, continually looked round for your countenance, and the name of Pudens was perpetually on my cold tongue. If the wool-spinning sisters do not weave the threads of my life back, and my voice does not address inattentive deities, you will return safe to the cities of Latium to see your

To Aulus Pudens.

friend safe, and as a deserving knight be rewarded with the rank of first centurion."

We learn from this and the following epigram that Pudens had not then reached the grade of a chief centurion, being simply a centurion, captain of one hundred men.

"Encolpus, the favourite of the centurion his master, consecrates these, the whole of the locks from his head, to thee, O Phœbus, when Pudens shall have gained the pleasing honour of the chief centurionship, which he has so well merited" (i. 31). *To Apollo.*

Probably on the capture of Caractacus he gained his promotion, and was one of those selected to accompany the illustrious prisoners on their long road, which he would shorten with many attentions to his captives, and thus the intimacy between himself and Claudia ripened into love. After their arrival in Rome the captives were liberated, and Claudia and Pudens were married, which is thus announced by Martial, 53 A.D. :—

"Claudia Peregrina Rufus is about to be married to my friend Pudens. Be propitious, Hymen, with thy torches. As fitly is precious cinnamon united with nard, and Massic wine with Attic honey. Nor are elms more fitly wedded to tender vines, the lotus more love the waters, or the myrtle the river's bank. Mayest thou always hover over their conch, fair Concord; and may Venus ever be auspicious to a couple so well matched. In after years may the wife cherish her husband in his old age; and may she, when grown old, not seem so to her husband" (iv. 13). *On the marriage of Pudens and Claudia.*

The young couple were soon surrounded with a family, two sons and two daughters—Novatus, Timotheus, Pudentiana, and Praxedes. On the birth of the third, Pudentiana, Martial again strikes his lyre, in the following beautiful and highly complimentary epigram (xi. 53) :—

"Although Claudia Rufina may be a blue-eyed Briton born, how much has she of the disposition of the Latin race! What a graceful figure! The Italian matrons might believe her a Roman, those of Attica of their country. The gods bless her, in that she proves fruitful to her pious husband. Therefore she may hope, as a young woman, to beget daughters-in-law. May it so please the powers that she rejoices in one husband for ever, and that she exult in three sons." *On Claudia Rufina.*

The wish that her third child may be a son is evidently expressed that she may enjoy the special privileges accorded to matrons having three male children. She was disappointed; the third was a girl.

Martial uses the phrase "pious husband" (*sancto marito*). May not this refer to his being a Christian? Paul, in writing to the Romans, calls him "the chosen in the Lord." He was probably a convert of St. Paul's disciples Aquila and Priscilla.

About this time, 58 A.D., Caractacus and his family returned to Britain, leaving behind Claudia and his second son, her brother Linus—they having all become Christians. It was doubtless Caractacus who first carried Christianity into Britain. The probability is that he was accompanied on his return to Britain by Aristobulus, said by the Greek Church to be the father-in-law of St. Peter. His name-day is March 15th. When St. Paul wrote to the Romans in 58 A.D. (xvi. 10), the year Caractacus went back, he salutes those which are of the household of Aristobulus, but not Aristobulus himself; doubtless he knew of his absence from Rome, and so greets his household only.

St. Paul, writing to the Romans about this time, sends greetings from Corinth to the Christians in Rome, enumerating several by name; amongst others, he says, "Salute Rufus, the chosen in the Lord, and his mother and mine" (Rom. xvi. 13).

Paul's mother and half-brother. The question here arises, Was this Rufus Pudens? If so, was he half-brother to Paul? Paul was born at Tarsus, and although his father was a Pharisee, his mother may have been a Roman. She, on the death of her husband, returned to Rome, and there married the Roman Pudentinus, and thus became the mother of Pudens, who was consequently the half-brother of St. Paul. It has been handed down by Hermes, and is the tradition of the Roman Church, that her Christian name was Priscilla. We see by verses 7 and 11 that Paul had kinsmen, Andronicus, Junia, and Herodion, in Rome. In A.D. 62 Paul is brought a prisoner to Rome, and "dwelt two whole years in his own hired house;" and in 64 he suffered martyrdom in the persecution under Nero. During these two years Paul would naturally be a frequent visitor at the house of his half-brother, whose family would comfort him in his last hours; and he writes to Timothy, "Eubulus greeteth thee, and Pudens, and Linus, and Claudia, and all the brethren" (2 Tim. iv. 21).

Between that time and his leaving Rome, Martial addresses the following epigrams to Pudens (vii. 11) :—

"You urge me, Pudens, to correct my books for you with my own hand and pen. You are far too partial and too kind thus to wish to possess my trifles in autograph." *To Aulus Pudens.*

> "The number of my books does them much wrong,
> The reader's tired and glutted with their throng:
> Scarce things take most, first fruits are nice,
> Roses in winter bear the highest price.
> Persius' one book is more celebrated far
> Than Marsus' bulky Amazonian War.
> Reading a book of mine, feign there is no more,
> Thus of my wit thou'lt make the greater store" (iv. 29).—*Anon.*, 1695.

The tradition of the Roman Church is that the house of Pudens was the hospice for all Christian visitors to Rome—a protection and hospitality he could well afford from his position and wealth. In this Christian centre and home Pudens founded an oratory or chapel, of which Hermes was the pastor. Paul says, "Salute Asyncritus, Phlegon, Hermas, Patrobas, Hermes, and the brethren which are with them" (Rom. xvi. 14).   *House of Pudens.*

This oratory is below the present Church of Sta. Pudentiana. Pudens died about 96 A.D. About this time John wrote his Second Epistle, in which he "exhorteth a certain honourable matron, with her children, to persevere in Christian love and belief." May not this epistle have been addressed to Claudia by St. John? These words would help to console her in her affliction. It applies to her exactly. Claudia followed Pudens to eternal life one year after, in 97.   *First church.*

Of their daughters we have some interesting details handed down by one Pastor, the priest, probably the son of the Hermes mentioned above, who took the name Pastor, or the Shepherd, from a work he wrote entitled "The Shepherd." He says: "The daughters of Pudens desired to have a baptistery in their house, and Pius (the bishop) drew the plan of the foundation. Their Christian slaves were declared free in the oratory founded by Pudens, and ninety-six neophytes were baptized at Easter. Henceforth constant services were held in the said oratory, the bishop Pius frequently visiting them. When Pudentiana went to God, we concealed her body twenty-eight days in the oratory, and then buried her near her father Pudens in the tomb of Priscilla. After eleven months Novatus died and left his goods to Praxedes, and she begged Pius to erect a church (*titular*) in the Baths of Novatus, which were no longer used, and where there was a large and spacious hall. The bishop made the dedication   *First baptistery.*   *Second church.*

in the name of the blessed virgin Pudentiana. In the same place he consecrated a baptistery" (Letter of Hermes).

This account of the building of this church is confirmed by Bishop Damasus in his works, edited by Anastasius. He says, "Pius (bishop) made a church in the Thermae of Novatus, and dedicated it in honour of his (Novatus') sister Pudentiana."

Does archaeology bear out any of the foregoing facts? is the question we have now to consider. What remains have we of the house of Pudens, his oratory, the baptistery, the Baths of Novatus, and the church dedicated by Pius? Let us see.

Archaeological evidence.

It has been faithfully handed down that these buildings were on the Vicus Patricius, which street is now known as the Via Urbana.

Remains.

Under the buildings on the left hand side, in going towards the Piazza dell' Esquilino, are considerable remains of what was evidently a large Roman house, the construction being of the first century, with repairs and alterations of the second. These remains can be visited by descending into the cellars of the different houses. Part of it is shown on the marble plan of Rome in the Capitoline Museum. Below the present Church of Sta. Pudentiana is a large hall divided by arch-pierced walls into two naves and two aisles, the construction of which is of the first century. The vaults have traces of stucco ornamentation, and the walls are decorated with the remains of frescoes within red bands or borders; the windows which once gave light to the building are now closed up; and the chambers are partly filled up with soil thrown in, probably, when the upper church was rebuilt. This we may look upon as the oratory founded by Pudens and recorded by Hermes. At the end of the east nave is a small square chamber, still containing remains of decoration, and having a mosaic pavement of white and black marble: here we have the baptistery mentioned above, as built by the two sisters after their father's death, designed by Pius, and where their ninety-six Christian slaves received baptism after their freedom.

The actual date of the erection of the Baths of Novatus is not known, but the construction of the remains agrees with the time of Domitian. At this time the level of the Vicus Patricius was raised, and upon its line, and consequently above part of the paternal house, and over that part containing the oratory and baptistery, the thermae were built, the old lower chambers being used as the necessary underground parts of the baths. Of this there is ample archaeological evidence in the hot-air flues cut into the brickwork of the first century. Novatus was martyred one year after Pudentiana, probably 108 A.D., and left the property to his sister Praxedes; and at her wish Pius turned the "large and spacious hall of the thermæ, which were no longer used, into a church."

The archæological witness of this is not to be shaken: at the back of the present church the end wall of the large hall still stands, showing construction of the time of Domitian.

In this wall were large windows which gave light to the original hall: these are filled up with second century brickwork, showing construction of the Antonines (98–169), agreeing with the date of Bishop Pius, who died 158, by whom the church was made. To this date may likewise be assigned the strengthening brick arches in the vaults below, erected to sustain the extra weight put upon the original arches. This church, as we have seen, was dedicated to Pudentiana,* and is sometimes mentioned in the early writers as Titulus Pudentis, and is so called in the Acts of the Synod held in Rome in 499, where is mentioned Asterius Justinus Presbyter, Tituli Pudentis. The Titulus Pudentis is spoken of in an inscription, dated 528, found in 1883 in the catacombs of St. Hippolitus. Anastasius so calls it, and says it had fallen into ruins, and was rebuilt by Hadrian I., 772–795, when the present apse with its mosaic was built inside the end wall of the great hall, the space so divided off forming a sacristy; and some of the arches of the lower church were walled up, as they show construction of the eighth century. Some explorations have recently been made in the house and church of Pudens, and a great deal of the earth removed. Several rooms of the house, part of the paved street, a portion of a beautiful mosaic floor of the church, part of the grinding cone of a mill, bricks stamped with the names of M. Flavius Aper (consul in 130), Q. Servilius, Q. F. Pudens (consul in 166), and of Septimius Severus, also some with first-century marks, have been brought to light. Above one of the arches of the east aisle a ninth-century fresco, representing St. Peter between SS. Pudentiana and Praxedes, was uncovered. All three figures have the nimbus, and their names are written vertically at their sides. St. Peter holds the keys in his left hand; upon his cloak are the initials of the artist. Both sisters hold a crown and veil in their left hands. St. Pudentiana holds a Latin cross in her right hand, whilst St. Praxedes has a maniple passed between her first and second fingers.

* A Leopardus, lletor of Pudentiana, is mentioned in an inscription dated 384.

The church dedicated to the elder of the two sisters stands back from the Via Urbana, on the slope of the Viminal Hill, and is below the modern level, the road having been raised in 1872. The present front is a restoration of Cardinal Buonaparte's; but the doorway is eighth century, sculpture work of that period.

The Church of Sta. Pudentiana, second century.

On the lintel in the centre is a medallion of the Lamb on the rock, from which flow the four rivers. On its left are Timotheus and Pudentiana, and on the right Praxedes and Novatus, the children of Rufus Pudens and Claudia.

The campanile, or bell-tower, is of the thirteenth century, and well preserved. The church now belongs to the nuns of the Augustine order.

On the right wall in entering the church is a painting representing the baptism of Pudens by Paul and Peter, by Reti. Beyond is an inscription speaking of the church as the oldest in Rome. This is a mistake, the oldest church being below the present one; but that was not known till discovered by the late Mr. John Henry Parker of Oxford in 1870.

Over the altar in the first chapel, on the right, is the Guardian Angel, signed, "D. Francisci Antonii Lelii de Fundi, 1618." The angel and child are very beautiful. The next chapel contains, over the altar, a Byzantine Madonna and Child. On the right wall is the Birth of the Virgin Mary, and on the left that of the Redeemer, both by Baldi. On the left in entering is the Virgin, and on the right the Angel of the Annunciation. In the adjoining chapel above the altar is the Virgin and St. Bernard. On the right is St. Bernard before the Almighty; on the left, Sta. Theresa receiving the Sacred Heart from the Saviour. The reference on the book is from Ecclesiasticus vi., "Come unto her with thy whole heart, and keep her ways with all thy power." These paintings are the works of M. Cippitelli, 1738.

The end chapel is dedicated to S. Pudens, and is still paved with its ancient mosaic. The painting over the altar is his baptism, by A. Nucci. On the left wall is a fragment of a Christian sarcophagus of the fourth century. It is divided into panels by composite columns, from which spring arches. Under the second arch is the sacred monogram. Below it are birds, beneath which is a cross, on either side of which is a soldier. On each side are a man and woman carrying wreaths.

On the left wall in entering is a painting of the two sisters collecting the remains of the martyrs, by Reti. Beyond is an inscription relating to the early history of the church. From the vault of the nave is suspended the hat of Cardinal Wiseman, who took his title from this church. The church is built in the form of a basilica, and was made out of the great hall of the Baths of Novatus in the time of Pius I. Pope Hadrian I. shortened the nave by inserting the apse, and built the piers round the columns which divided the nave from the aisles. The altar-piece represents the Assumption of Sta. Pudentiana, whilst on the sides are Timotheus and Novatus, the works of Bernardino Nocchi of Lucca. Above is the Byzantine mosaic of Hadrian I., 772-795. It represents our Saviour seated. In his hand is an open book, on which is written, " Dominus Conservator Ecclesiæ Pudentianæ." On either side are SS. Paul and Peter, with several members of the family of Pudens. The two sisters are represented behind the apostles, and about to place wreaths over their heads. In the background is a wall having several gates, and over the wall are buildings, probably those of the palace of Pudens.* Above are the jewelled cross and the beasts from Revelation. The dome above the chancel is frescoed by Pomarancio. In the centre is the head of the Saviour, surrounded by the heavenly choir; below, in front, are Paul, Peter, and Pudens; on the right are the two brothers, and on the left the two sisters. The left aisle runs back beyond the apse to the original end wall, and is paved with the old mosaic work. At its end is the altar of St. Peter, within which is preserved one of the sponges used by the sisters in collecting the blood of the martyrs. Above the altar is a life-like representation of Christ giving the keys to Peter (Matt. xvi. 19)—"I will give unto thee the keys of the kingdom of heaven." It is by G. B. della Porta, 1570, the masterpiece of this master, and a real work of art. On the right, built into the wall, is a marble slab, said to be the table top on which St. Peter celebrated the Lord's Supper when staying in the house of Pudens. The frescoes on the roof above refer to scenes in the life of St. Peter, and are by Baglioni. On the left hand wall is a copy of an inscription of Hadrian I., and one from the catacombs

---

* Siricius, the Bishop, and Valerius Messala, the Prefect, of Rome, made a portico 1,000 feet long in the Vicus Patricius in 398. This is perhaps represented in the background of the mosaic, which some authorities think is of their time. Gruter (clxxiv. 9) gives the following inscription relating to repairs on the Vicus Patricius made by the Prefect of Rome in the time of Arcadius and Honorius, 395-408:—

FLAVIVS . VAL . MESSALA . V . C . PRAEFECTVS .
VRBI . SPLENDOREM . PVBLICVM . IN VICO PATRICIO
VICTORIAE . ET . FIERI . ET . ORNARI . PROCVRAVIT .

of S. Priscilla relative to a member of the family of Pudens. Halfway down this aisle is the beautiful chapel of the Gaetani family, built by Cardinal Gaetani in 1597, Francesco da Volterra being the architect.

At the entry are four veneered Corinthian columns of Numidian marble. The roof was designed by F. Zuccari, and executed in Byzantine mosaic by P. Rossetto, 1600. In the centre is the Holy Dove, and at the spandrels the Four Evangelists. Over the door are the two sisters collecting the blood and the remains of the martyrs. On the left is the tomb of Don Enrico, the founder of the chapel, and on the right Don Philippo Gaetani. The windows of coloured glass represent S. Pudentiana on the right,* and the crucifixion above the altar. On the right is a statue of Fortune by Guidi, Temperance by A. Lorenese; on the left, Justice by Carlo Malavista, and Prudence by F. Mari. The chapel is decorated with the most beautiful ancient marbles—verde antico, alabaster, porta santa, pietra pidocchio, breccia nero, etc. The altar-piece is the finest work of its class in Rome—a high relief in white marble, the masterpiece of Peter Paul Olivieri (1551–91), representing the Adoration of the Magi. There is nothing forced or theatrical in this beautiful work of art; it is natural and life-like, the seated mother and Child being most natural. On either side of the altar is a column of Sicilian jasper, with bronze gilt vases and capitals, said to have been brought from the Temple of Jupiter Capitolinus.

The church dedicated to the sister saint (*Church of S. Praxedes*) is on the Esquiline Hill, near S. Maria Maggiore. It has nothing to do with the saint personally, but a description of it will be found in our "Rambles in Rome."

* This stained-glass window was unfortunately damaged in the explosion of April 23, 1891.

VII.

WORK AND DEATH.

SOME idea of how St. Paul spent the two years in Rome before his death may be gleaned from his letters. He not only established the church there, and preached the gospel, but directed many affairs of the churches of his foundation in other parts; and so the time would quickly pass away. During this time St. Luke seems to have been the constant companion of St. Paul, and to have occupied himself in writing the *St. Luke.* Acts of the Apostles and his Gospel. St. Paul, at liberty to move about the city as he pleased, made many converts, not only among the citizens, but also in the Prætorian Camp and in the Imperial Palace itself. Writing to the Philippians (ch. i. 12, 13), he says, "But I would ye should understand, *Soldiers and imperial servants converts.* brethren, that the things which happened unto me have fallen out rather unto the furtherance of the gospel; so that my bonds in Christ are manifest in all the Prætorium, and in all other places." And in ch. iv. 22: "All the saints salute you, chiefly they that are of Cæsar's household." His mixing so much with the soldiers gave him the idea of his beautiful allegory of a *Christian's armour.* Christian's armour (Eph. vi. 13; 1 Thess. v. 8); and he often speaks of his fellow-labourers as fellow-soldiers. So the crowding of the people to the games of the circus suggests the race of a Christian life, and he compares himself to a runner: "Let us run with patience the race that is set before us" (Heb. xii. 1); and Phil. iii. 13, 14: "Forgetting those things which are behind, and reaching

CIRCUS MAXIMUS.
(*From a Coin.*)

Races.

forth unto those things which are before, I press toward the goal for the prize of the high calling of God in Christ Jesus." He had used this simile before in writing to the Corinthians (1 Cor. ix. 24–27), and it was a good illustration to them, who were so familiar with the stadium: "Know ye not that they which run in a race run all, but one receiveth the prize? So run, that ye may obtain. And every man that striveth for the mastery is temperate in all things. Now they do it to obtain a corruptible crown; but we an incorruptible. I therefore so run, not as uncertainly; so fight I, not as one that beateth the air: but I keep under my body, and bring it into subjection." And in writing to his beloved Timothy, just before his death, he says, "I have finished my course" (2 Tim. iv. 7). The reports he receives of the Philippians, and their gift (Phil. iv. 18),

Epaphroditus. pleased him; and the care of their messenger Epaphroditus, who fell sick, is simply but beautifully touched upon. Knowing that the churches thought of him and prayed for

Onesiphorus. him cheered him in his captivity; whilst the visit of Onesiphorus must indeed have been to him a bright time. "He oft refreshed me, and was not ashamed of my chain: but, when he was in Rome, he sought me out very diligently, and found

Onesimus. me" (2 Tim. i. 16, 17). Amidst all these scenes, the conversion of the runaway slave Onesimus, and St. Paul's love for him, is full of touching pathos. Onesimus had run away from his master Philemon at Colosse, after robbing him, and had taken refuge in that great city where all the bad seem to have found asylum. There, in some way, he meets with St. Paul: probably he had heard him preach when with his master; perhaps conscience smote him, and he confessed his faults. The apostle talks to him; he is converted, and becomes "a faithful and beloved brother;" and after a time Paul sends him back to his master with a touching letter, in which he generously offers to pay anything his convert had taken, and to bear the wrong done to Philemon.

Prepares for his trial. At length the Emperor Nero, it is rumoured, is about to return to Rome, and the great apostle prepares for the hearing of his appeal, and he seems confident of being released and set at liberty.

Timotheus "therefore I hope to send presently, so soon as I shall see how it will go with me. But I trust in the Lord that I also

Hopes of release. myself shall come shortly" (Phil. ii. 23, 24). "And having this confidence, I know that I shall abide and continue with you all for your furtherance and joy of faith;

that your rejoicing may be more abundant in Jesus Christ for me by my coming to you again" (i. 25, 26). And in his epistle to Philemon he says (ver. 22): "But withal prepare me also a lodging: for I trust that through your prayers I shall be given unto you." In his second epistle to Timothy he invites him to come to him: "Do thy diligence to come shortly unto me"—"Do thy diligence to come before winter" (iv. 9, 21). He likewise tells him to bring Mark with him (ver. 11); also "the cloke that I left at Troas with Carpus, when thou comest bring with thee, and the books, but especially the parchments" (ver. 13). These he had left behind when he walked from Troas to Assos. In parting with his friends at Miletus, he seems to have had a presentiment that he should never return; for he says: "And now, behold, I know that ye all, among whom I have gone preaching the kingdom of God, shall see my face no more" (Acts xx. 25). "Sorrowing most of all for the words which he spake, that they should see his face no more. And they accompanied him unto the ship" (ver. 38).

In closing his second letter to Timothy, he complains that at his first trial, at Cæsarea, no friend was with him, and that he stood alone. He says: "At my first answer no man stood with me, but all men forsook me: I pray God that it may not be laid to their charge. Notwithstanding the Lord stood with me......that by me the preaching might be fully known, and that all the Gentiles might hear: and I was delivered out of the mouth of the lion"—the tribe of Judah, the Jews—(iv. 16, 17). "Judah is a lion's whelp" (Gen. xlix. 9). "As a young lion to the house of Judah" (Hosea v. 14). "The Lion of the tribe of Juda" (Rev. v. 5). The like figurative language is used when he speaks of fighting with wild beasts at Ephesus (1 Cor. xv. 32). The Ephesians were the wild beasts. David says (Ps. xxii. 21): "Save me from the lion's mouth." (See the parable of the lion in Ezekiel xix. 1-9.) The word "lion" was used by the Jews to express a tyrant or enemy. "Marsyas, the freedman of Agrippa, informed him of the death of Tiberius by saying in Hebrew, 'The lion is dead'" (Josephus, "A.," xviii. 17). And Esther says (xiv. 13): "Give me eloquent speech in my mouth before the Lion." So Ignatius calls the soldiers who guarded him ten leopards ("Ep. to Romans," v.).

First Trial.

Now the members of the Christian church in Rome were with him, "Eubulus, Pudens, Linus, Claudia, and all the brethren;" but of the old companions he says, "Only Luke is with me" (ver. 11). He is fully prepared for his

Not alone now.

trial, as appears by his letter to the Philippians (i. 20, 21) : " According to my earnest expectation and my hope, that in nothing I shall be ashamed, but that with all boldness, as always, so now also Christ shall be magnified in my body, whether it be by life, or by death. For to me to live is Christ, and to die is gain."

Paul is now prepared for the emperor's coming; but on the night of May 19th, 64 A.D., a terrible fire broke out, which lasted many days, and destroyed the best part of the city of Rome.

Burning of Rome.

"There being near his palace some granaries, the site of which he exceedingly coveted, they were battered as if with machines of war, and set on fire, the walls being built of stone. During six days and seven nights this terrible devastation continued, the people being obliged to fly to the tombs and monuments for lodging and shelter. This fire he beheld from a tower in the villa of Mæcenas, and 'being greatly delighted,' as he said, 'with the beautiful effects of the conflagration,' he sang a poem on the ruin of Troy, in the tragic dress he used on the stage" (Suetonius, "Nero," xxxviii.).

"He set on fire the city of Rome, that he might enjoy the sight of a spectacle such as Troy formerly presented when taken and burned" (Eutropius, vii. 14).

"Nero sent some men privately, who pretended to be drunk or mad. They first set fire to one place, then to several, so that the inhabitants were in an incredible consternation......This deplorable misfortune continued several days and nights, during which abundance of houses were consumed for want of succour......Nero, dressed like a harper, was at the top of a tower in his palace, from whence he diverted himself with the sight of the fire, and as it burned he sang songs that had been made on the taking of Troy, and which agreed yet better with the destruction of Rome. This city had never suffered before or since any accident so fatal, except when it was burned by the Gauls" (Dion Cassius, lxii. 16, etc.).

"There followed a terrible disaster, whether fortuitously or by the wicked contrivance of the prince is not determined, for both are asserted by historians; but of all the calamities which ever befell this city from the rage of fire, this was the most terrible and severe. It broke out near that part of the circus which is contiguous to Mounts Palatine and Cœlian, where, by reason of shops in which were kept such goods as minister aliment to fire, the moment it commenced it acquired strength, and being accelerated by the wind, it spread at once through the whole extent of the circus. For neither were the houses secured by enclosures nor the temples environed with walls, nor was there any other obstacle to intercept its progress; but the flames, spreading every way impetuously, invaded first the lower regions of the city, then mounted to the higher; then again ravaging the lower, they baffled every effort to extinguish them by the rapidity of their destructive course, and from the liability of the city to conflagration in consequence of the narrow and intricate alleys and the irregularity of the streets in ancient Rome" (Tacitus, "A.," xv. 38).

"When the fire broke out Nero was at Antium, and did not return to the city till the fire had approached that quarter of his house which connected the palace with the villa of Mæcenas; nor could it, however, be prevented from devouring the house and palace and everything around. A rumour had become universally current that at the very time when the city was in flames, Nero, going on the stage of his private theatre, sang *The Destruction of Troy*, assimilating the present disaster to that catastrophe of ancient times" (xxxix.). "At length, on the sixth day, the conflagration was stayed at the foot of the Esquiliæ" (xl.). "There are some who remark that the commencement of this fire showed itself on the 14th before the kalends of the sixth month (May 19th), the day on which the Senones (Gauls) set fire to the captured city" (xli.).

In August 1888, in building the palace of the royal household on the west side of the Church of S. Andrea al Quirinale, in the cellar of the palace an altar was discovered of considerable interest, as it is connected with the fire under Nero.

A newly-discovered record of the fire.

The street now called Via del Quirinale was anciently the Alta Semita or High Street, fronting on to the ancient level of which, and reached by descending three steps, a paved area was found, in the centre of which is an altar elevated on two steps. The pavement of the area and the altar are in travertine stone, but the altar was once cased with marble. The paved area has been traced under the front of the palace for 40 feet; and along the line of the bottom step were a series of boundary posts, in travertine, with their tops shaped like a pyramid. The altar is 10 feet in front by 20½ feet deep and 4½ feet high, and can be seen by descending into the cellar.

We give the following translation, as it is not recorded by any historian:—

"This enclosed area, truly defined with boundary stones, and the altar which is below, is dedicated by Imperial Cæsar, Domitian Augustus, a vow taken upon himself by Germanicus, which had been for a long time neglected and unredeemed, as an incentive to keep off fires, when the city burned for nine days in the time of Nero. By this decree it is dedicated that it is not lawful for any one to erect edifices within these bounds, nor for dealers to remain there, neither to plant trees nor to sow any other thing. And the prætor or any other magistrate to whom this region by chance falls is to celebrate the ceremonies on the Volcanalia, on the tenth day before the kalends of September (August 23) every year, by sacrificing a red heifer and a boar, with the imprecations written below, which the Imperial Cæsar, Domitian Augustus Germanicus, High Priest, constitutes as a festival" (Gruter, lxi. 3; C. I. L., 826).

In A.D. 84, Domitian undertook an expedition into Germany, and returned to Rome without seeing the enemy; and so he took the name of Germanicus. It was probably on the dedication of this altar that Martial wrote the epigram to Vulcan(v.7),so that it was erected after 84.

The Festival of Vulcan was held in the Circus Maximus, and Dion Cassius (lxxviii. 25) describes how Macrinus wished to abolish the games in the year 217 A.D., when on the festival, August 23rd, the Colosseum was ruined by an earthquake, and the upper gallery, which was of wood, fired by a thunderbolt. The god thus *apropos* showed his wrath.

The first day of the month was the kalends, and they reckoned it in their calculation, so the 14th before the kalends of June, sixth month, would be the 19th not 18th of May.

Livy (vi. 1) says the Battle of the Allia occurred on the day previous to the 15th before the kalends of the sixth month. Of the time Livy was writing, the sixth month was August; so, according to him, the battle took place on the 17th July. The Gauls entered Rome the next day, and fired it on the day following. This does not agree with the above quotation from Tacitus, for when he was writing, the sixth month was June. Julius Cæsar changed the first month from March to January. July was so called from Julius Cæsar, and August from Augustus Cæsar. The only way to reconcile the statements of Livy and Tacitus is to conclude that Livy gives the date from the new style, although speaking of an event under the old style. If Tacitus is dating after the old style, although relating an event which took place under the new style, the fire broke out on July 17th. This would not agree with the Church of Rome, which says St. Paul suffered on the 29th of June; whereas, if the fire started, as Tacitus says, fourteen days before the commencement of the sixth month, May 19th, the stricter guarding of the apostle would take place, and Paul might well have suffered on the 29th of

June. That would give just over a month for the agitation to be got up against the Christians, for Paul to be under close arrest (during which he wrote his second epistle to Timothy), and then for the active persecution to break out, culminating in the death of St. Paul and his fellow-Christians in the Circus of Nero.

There is no doubt that by the orders of Nero the city was fired, and to escape the odium and murmurs of the people he threw the blame upon the Christians, and the consequence was that a persecution against them broke out, and many suffered martyrdom. Paul, under surveillance, and now the well-known leader of the Christians in Rome, would be one of the first to *First persecution.*

NERO AND POPPÆA.

be seized upon. He speaks of this in writing at this time to Timothy (2 Tim. ii. 9): "I suffer hardship unto bonds, as a malefactor;" and now, under the old charge and supposed new offence, he was condemned to death. We have no particulars of the trial, but the historian Tacitus gives us a graphic description of how and where the Christians suffered; and as in Roman jurisprudence there was no time allowed between sentence and execution, as in the case of our Saviour, who was led from the judgment-hall to crucifixion, and Stephen from the court of the high priest to be stoned (see Tacitus, "A.," iii. 51, vi. 19, 39, 40), so St. Paul, not being condemned to imprisonment but to death, was led from the judgment-hall to suffer with the members of his flock in the Circus of Nero, in his gardens *Trial.*

Paul condemned.

on the Vatican Hill, as described by Tacitus ; which spot is now occupied by the Cathedral of St. Peter's, thus forming a grand monument to the first martyrs in Rome.

"Hence, to suppress the rumour, he falsely charged with the guilt, and punished with the most exquisite tortures, the persons commonly called Christians, who were hated for their enormities [being mixed up by the Romans with the Jews, who at this time were in revolt]. Christus, the founder of that name, was put to death as a criminal by Pontius Pilate, procurator of Judea, in the reign of Tiberius ; but the pernicious superstition, repressed for a time, broke out again, not only throughout Judea, where the mischief originated, but through the city of Rome also, whither all things horrible and disgraceful flow, from all quarters, as to a common receptacle, and where they are encouraged. Accordingly, first those were seized who confessed they were Christians ; next, on their information, a vast multitude were convicted, not so much on the charge of burning the city, as of hating the human race. And in their deaths they were also made the subjects of sport ; for they were covered with the hides of wild beasts and worried to death by dogs, or nailed to crosses, or set fire to, and when day declined, burned to serve for nocturnal lights. Nero offered his own gardens for that spectacle, and exhibited a circensian game, indiscriminately mingling with the common people in the habit of a charioteer, or else standing in his chariot ; whence a feeling of compassion arose towards the sufferers, though guilty and deserving to be made examples of by capital punishment, because they seemed not to be cut off for the public good, but victims to the ferocity of one man" ("Annals," xv. 44).

The *tunica molesta* (pitched shirt), as a means of punishment, is spoken of by several of the Roman authors. (See Martial, x. 25 ; Juvenal, i. 155, viii. 235.) Suetonius ("Nero," xvi.) says, "He likewise inflicted punishments on the Christians, a sort of people who held a new and impious superstition."

Amidst the ruins of the palace of Domitian, on the Palatine Hill, are the ruins of a basilica or hall of justice. The buildings of Domitian occupy an artificial platform, which was formed after the fire in the reign of Titus, when the Palace of Augustus and adjacent buildings were destroyed. The ruins were filled in by Domitian, and on the top he erected his palace. Some of the buildings so filled up were consecrated, and consequently had to be rebuilt at the higher level. One so treated

The Basilica.

is the Hall of Justice, which, there is evidence, was erected on the lines of the older one. As this is the only basilica on the Palatine, we may fairly presume that here the appeals unto Cæsar were heard by the emperor in person, and that in the older building below the present level St. Paul was condemned by Nero, 64 A.D.

The remains consist of a very wide nave with narrow aisles ; the tribunal, with a piece of the judge's chair ; a portion of the cancelli rail ; fragments of the columns which supported the galleries ; and part of the pavement, consisting of the round stone on which the prisoner stood to be tried.

Well might the great apostle exclaim prophetically, in writing to Timothy, "for I am now ready to be offered, and the time of my departure is at hand. I have fought a good fight, I have finished my course, I have kept the faith : henceforth there is laid up for me a crown of righteousness, which the Lord, the righteous judge, shall give me at that day" (2 Tim. iv. 6-8). *Prepared.*

Suetonius ("Nero," xv.) says, "In the administration of justice, he scarcely ever gave his decision on the pleadings before the next day, and then in writing. His manner of hearing causes was not to allow any adjournment, but to despatch them in order as they stood. When he withdrew, he consulted his assessors. He did not debate the matter openly with them, but silently and privately reading over their opinions, which they gave separately in writing, he pronounced sentence from the tribunal according to his own view of the case, as if it were the opinion of the majority." *How Nero dispensed judgment.*

VIII.

A SILENT WITNESS.

IN the centre of Nero's Circus, upon the spina, stood an Egyptian obelisk, brought over from the quarries (never having been erected in Egypt) by Caligula. This is the sole witness of the death of these heroic Christians. It now stands in front of St. Peter's in Rome, having been removed from its original site (to the

ST. PETER'S, AND OBELISK.

left of the church—the place bears an inscription) in 1586. This monument reminds us of their sufferings and glory, of which it is before God and man a silent witness. It bears the inscription— "Christ is triumphant! Christ reigns! Christ is Emperor! Christ paid all our debts!"

IX.

ST. PAUL'S EPISTLES FROM ROME.

IN studying the history of St. Paul considerable difficulty is encountered from the way or order in which the letters are placed in our Bibles, as likewise from the erroneous dates at the head of the epistles, and the equally false subscriptions. People who have written about the history of St. Paul have taken these dates and subscriptions as facts, and consequently many have been led into error and romance, whilst no end of confusion and false ideas has resulted. Of the dates given only one is correct—that to the Galatians. Many places are ascribed wrongly as the place of writing. One place is mentioned—Laodicea—which St. Paul never visited; and one letter, that to Titus, is said to have been written from a place that never existed—Nicopolis of Macedonia. The letters are also said to have been written by certain people who were simply the carriers of the letters; and one in which Paul says, "I Paul have written it with my own hand," is said to have been written by the servant of him to whom it is addressed.

We have attempted to put all this jumble and confusion straight, and append a table showing the order, time, place of writing, by whom addressed, and by whom the correspondence of St. Paul was carried, dwelling more particularly on those written from Rome.

After the apostle had comfortably settled down in his own hired house, he writes his first epistle from Rome—that to the Colossians—in the autumn of 62. He speaks of "our brother" Timotheus; Epaphras, who had evidently recently arrived from Colosse; Onesimus, whom he had converted, and was sending with Tychicus to Colosse; Luke, and other fellow-workers; but he is not so full of his own troubles as later on. In the last chapter he says, "for which I am also in bonds" (ver. 3), and "Remember my bonds." In the supposed companion epistle to the Laodiceans he says, "And my bonds are manifested which I suffer in Christ."

Summer of 62 to Summer of 64.

Epistle to the Colossians, written from Rome, 62.

The epistle to Philemon begins in the same way as the above in coupling the name of Timotheus with that of Paul. It is written to the master of Onesimus, for whom it pleads. In it Paul speaks of himself as aged and a prisoner, *and also* Epaphras, whom he does not call a prisoner in the

Epistle to Philemon, written from Rome, 62.

former letter. Luke and the others send salutations; and Paul evidently does not expect to stay long in Rome, for he says, "But withal prepare me a lodging." He found the Romans, as we do, slow to action. He speaks of Mark and Luke being with him (ver. 24). It is evident that these two letters were written about the same time.

After being in Rome a short time, and no accusation being sent *Epistle to Titus, written from Rome, 63.* from Jerusalem against him, he evidently thinks of being released, and writes to Titus, whom he had left in Crete on his journey to Rome (Titus i. 5): "When I shall send Artemas unto thee, or Tychicus, be diligent to come unto me to Nicopolis: for I have determined there to winter" (iii. 12). This city of Nicopolis was on the coast of Epirus, visited when going to Illyricum (Rom. xv. 19). He was not at Nicopolis when he wrote, "I have determined there to winter." If he had been there he would have said "here." He calls Titus his son (ver. 4), as he does Timothy, and has made him likewise a bishop, and in this letter addresses to him advice similar to that which he gave to Timothy. In the whole of this epistle he does not say a word about bonds or captivity.

In the following letter we see he has lost his hope of liberty, and sends Tychicus to Ephesus. In his second epistle to Timothy, Paul speaks of Titus as being in Dalmatia (iv. 10).

It is an old dispute whether the epistle to the Hebrews was written *Epistle to the Hebrews, written from Rome, 63.* by St. Paul or not. Origen says, "God only knows who wrote it. According to some, Clement, the bishop of Rome, wrote it; according to others, St. Luke" (Eusebius, "E. H.," vi. 25). But Clement asserts the epistle to the Hebrews was written by Paul in the Hebrew tongue, but that it was carefully translated by Luke, and published among the Greeks (Eusebius, vi. 14). As Clement was contemporary with St. Paul, we may conclude that he knew without doubt who was the author—namely, St. Paul.

In the thirteenth chapter he says, "Remember them that are in bonds" (ver. 3); and in ver. 19, "The rather to do this, that I may be restored to you the sooner." In the twenty-third verse we get a new piece of information—that Timotheus had been imprisoned. He says, "Know ye that our brother Timotheus is set at liberty; with whom, if he come shortly, I will see you." This incident in Timotheus's life seems to have taken place away from Rome, probably at Philippi (Phil. ii. 19); for Paul says, "if he come shortly"—that is, returns soon to Rome. The phrase, "I will see you," evidently springs from the idea that he will be released soon (Phile. 22; Titus iii. 12), which fixes the date of the letter in the early part of 63.

After being in Rome about a twelvemonth, Paul writes to the Ephesians, and sends the letter by Tychicus (Eph. vi. 21); and he confirms this in his second epistle to Timothy (iv. 12): "Tychicus have I sent to Ephesus." The apostle has already been under surveillance a year, and finds it irksome. In this epistle he constantly refers to his captivity. "I Paul, the prisoner of Jesus Christ for you Gentiles" (iii. 1); "I therefore, the prisoner of the Lord" (iv. 1); "I am an ambassador in bonds" (vi. 21). The soldiers had made him familiar with their arms and armour, hence the beautiful similitude in the last chapter.

Epistle to the Ephesians or Laodiceans, written from Rome, 63.

The epistles to the Colossians and Ephesians are parallel ones, like those to Timothy and Titus.

The epistle to the Philippians also comes from Paul and Timotheus (i. 1). Towards the close of the year 63 the apostle could look on his work in Rome as showing some result—"So that my bonds in Christ are manifest in all the Prætorian camp, and in all other places" (i. 13). "All the saints salute you, especially they that are of the household of Cæsar" (Nero)—iv. 22. Then he speaks of contention in the church of Rome (i. 14, 15, 16), and anticipates his death (i. 20, 21, ii. 17). He hopes to send Timotheus to Philippi (ii. 19), "as soon as I shall see how it will go with me" (ver. 23). This letter was an answer to the offerings they had sent him by Epaphroditus.

Epistle to the Philippians, written from Rome, 63.

The last of the Pauline epistles, the second to Timothy, was written from Rome just before his death in the great persecution under Nero. As far as we know, Paul had not seen his "beloved son" since he left him at Ephesus when he went into Macedonia in 58, unless Timothy was one of those who came to meet Paul at Miletus in 59. But now in 64 he was expecting his death. He was kept in stricter custody, as the Christians were in bad odour on account of the fire in Rome. Paul says, "I suffer trouble, as an evildoer, even unto bonds" (ii. 9). The Christians were charged with the evil deed of incendiarism; so Paul, their leader, was evidently looked close after. He expects the result, and is prepared—"For I am now ready to be offered, and the time of my departure is at hand" (iv. 6). At this crisis he naturally yearns towards his "beloved son," and writes his last words to him; and with the natural desire to see Timothy—"Greatly desiring to see thee" (2 Tim. i. 4)—after an absence of six years, says to him, "Do thy diligence to come shortly unto me." The hope of life

2nd Epistle to Timothy, written from Rome, May 64.

and work is yet within him; and so he asks for John Mark to be brought (Mark was with him in Rome in 62, and probably had been sent by him with the Hebrew epistle on his way to Colosse), his cloak that he had left five years before at Troas, and likewise the parchments. He writes of the principal events that had happened since he saw Timothy, and of the whereabouts of his fellow-labourers, saying that of them "only Luke is with me." He had sent Mark to the Colossians soon after his letter from Rome (Col. iv. 10).

He is very anxious for Timothy to come to him, for towards the close of his letter he says, "Do thy diligence to come before winter" (ver. 21). He had already passed two winters in Rome, and felt the want of his cloak, and so the bishop of Ephesus is asked to bring it as he passed by Troas.

As he pens his last words he naturally thinks of the trial before him, and dwells upon his former appearance before the judges. He says (ver. 16), "At my first answer no man stood with me, but all men forsook me." His first answer, three years before, had been at Cæsarea, before Festus the Roman governor (Acts xxv. 6). He could not say this in regard to Rome in the face of his previous assertion that Luke was with him, and that he was surrounded in Rome by converts, friends, and his kinsfolk Pudens, Linus, and Claudia. But at Cæsarea no one was with him; he stood alone when he appealed to Cæsar. "Notwithstanding," he says, "the Lord stood with me...that by me the preaching might be fully known, and that all the Gentiles might hear" (ver. 17). This was fulfilled. He preached in Rome, the capital and resort of the world, where people from all parts of the earth met, and doubtless heard him preach. Still, referring to his first trial at Cæsarea, he says, "And I was delivered out of the mouth of the lion." That expresses his deliverance exactly. The lion had watched him, shook him, worried him, and otherwise annoyed him; but as God had told him he was to bear witness also in Rome, God delivered him from the lion of Judah, the Jews who were persecuting him. He here calls the Jews a lion, as he had previously called the Ephesians wild beasts (1 Cor. xv. 32). Much of St. Paul's language was figurative, and the figure here was very apt.

In June 64, in the terrible persecution under Nero, the apostle, whose footsteps and letters we have traced, gained his crown of righteousness, most probably before Timothy and Mark could get to him, but the news of whose decease Mark carried to St. Peter (1 Pet. v. 13). According to tradition, Paul suffered on the twenty-ninth of the month.

ORDER OF THE EPISTLES.

Date.	Title.	By whom Addressed.	Where Written.	Authority.	By whom Carried.
53...	1st Thessalonians........	Paul, Silvanus, Timotheus..	Corinth ...	1 Thess. i. 7, 8; Acts xviii. 5.	Timotheus.
53....	2nd Thessalonians.......	Paul, Silvanus, Timotheus.	Corinth ...	Salutation by Paul............	
56....	1st Corinthians...........	Paul and Sosthenes........	Ephesus..	1 Cor. xvi. 8	Timothy and Titus.
58.....	2nd Corinthians	Paul and Timotheus........	Philippi..	2 Cor. i. 23, vii. 5.............	Titus, Luke, Timotheus.
58....	To Romans................	Paul.....................	Corinth ..	Rom. xv. 25, xvi. 23..........	Phebe.
58....	To Galatians..............	Paul.....................	Corinth ...	Acts xx. 2; Gal. vi. 11, v. 2..	
60....	1st Timothy...............	Paul.....................	Miletus ..	1 Tim. i. 3; Acts xx. 15......	
62.....	To Colossians.............	Paul and Timotheus........	Rome	A prisoner...................	Tychicus and Onesimus.
62.....	To Philemon..............	Paul and Timotheus	Rome	A prisoner...................	Tychicus and Onesimus.
62....	To Titus..................	Paul.....................	Rome	Compare with that to Timothy.	Zenas and Apollos (?).
63....	To Hebrews	Paul.....................	Rome	A prisoner...................	Mark (?).
63....	To Ephesians (Laodiceans)..	Paul.....................	Rome	A prisoner...................	Tychicus.
63....	To Philippians............	Paul and Timotheus........	Rome	A prisoner...................	Epaphroditus.
64....	2nd Timothy..............	Paul.....................	Rome	A prisoner...................	

DATES ARE STUBBORN FACTS.

To prove the correctness of the above dates, we append a chronological table, compiled from the historians Tacitus, Suetonius, Dion Cassius, and other classic authors, of the leading events in the life of Nero. The ancient Romans dated by consuls, which dates we and others have assimilated to our mode of reckoning, so that with certainty, without any doubt, the precise dates can be fixed. Nero was the son of Domitius Ahenobarbus Nero and Agrippina, the daughter of Germanicus.

37. Saulus Paulus converted, January 25th.

Nero was born at Antium, December 15th, nine months after the death of Tiberius.

49. Paul at Antioch.

Nero adopted by Claudius, his tutor being Seneca.

50. Paul goes to Jerusalem.

Afranius Burrhus appointed chief of the Prætorians by Claudius.

51. Paul visits Europe.

Caractacus brought a prisoner to Rome with his family.

53. Paul at Corinth.

Nero marries Octavia, the daughter of Claudius.

54. Paul returns to Antioch.

Nero succeeds Claudius at seventeen (in eighteenth year), October 13th.

57. Paul at Ephesus.

Pomponia Græcina (Gladys, sister of Caractacus), wife of Aulus Lateranus, tried for being a Christian. Acquitted.

59. Paul in Macedonia.

Nero murders his mother. Builds his circus at the Vatican. Riot at Pompeii.

60. Summer, Paul arrested at Jerusalem. Detained at Cæsarea.

A great comet appears. Josephus visits Rome for the first time.

61. Paul still detained at Cæsarea, but starts for Rome in the autumn.

Felix recalled. Revolt in Britain. London and Colchester burned. Ismael, the high priest of the Jews, and Helcias, keeper of the treasury, come on an embassy to Nero.

62. In the month of June, Paul arrives in Rome.

Persius the poet dies on November 24th. Nero, in the spring of the year, poisons Afranius Burrhus. He appoints two prefects as chiefs of the Prætorians—Fennius Rufus and Sophonius Tigellinus. Nero marries Poppæa Sabina, having divorced Octavia twelve days. Murders Octavia, June 9th.

63. "And Paul dwelt two whole years in his own hired house, and received all that came in unto him, preaching the kingdom of God, and teaching those things which concern the Lord Jesus Christ, with all confidence, no man forbidding him" (Acts xxviii. 30, 31).

64. St. Paul and his fellow-Christians put to death in the Circus of Nero at Mons Vaticanus on June 29th.

Earthquake at Pompeii. Poppæa confined at Antium of a daughter. Ambassadors come from Vologeses, king of Parthia. Nero gives extraordinary gladiatorial exhibitions.

Nero comes out on the stage at Naples. Revisits Rome. Attends the feast of Tigellinus. Goes to Antium. On the 19th of May, in the consulship of Caius Lecanius Bassus and Marcus Licinius Crassus Frugi, Rome is fired by the orders of Nero, who is at Antium. Returns to Rome on the sixth day of the fire (May 24th). Blames the Christians for the fire. Institutes a great persecution against the Christians, and puts them to death in his circus at the Vatican. Festus dies. Comet appears at the close of the year.

65. Conspiracy of Piso (April 15th). Seneca, Lucan, F. Rufus (prefect of the Prætorians), and Aulus Plautius Lateranus murdered.

66. Quinquennial games; visit of Tiridates. Kills his wife Poppæa by a kick. Junius Gallio put to death. Murders M. Vestinus Atticus the consul, and marries his wife Statilia Messalina. Petronius the author is with Nero at Cuma in the spring, when he is arrested and commits suicide. Annæus Mela put to death. In the early summer Nero goes to Greece and makes a theatrical tour. [M. Holleaux discovered in 1888 the speech made by Nero at Acræphia in Bœotia.]

67. In the autumn Nero returns to Rome and puts to death Thrasea Pætus, Bareas Soranus, and his daughter Servilia, who was a Christian.

68. On the 9th of June Nero attempts suicide, but is killed by his secretary Epaphroditus, "in the thirtieth year of his age and in the fourteenth of his reign" (Eutropius). "He lived thirty years and six months, having reigned thirteen years and eight months" (Dion Cassius). "He died in the thirty-first year of his age" (Suetonius).

It will be seen from the above dates that during the summers of 66 and 67 Nero was absent in Greece, so Paul could not have stood before him in Rome in the June of either of those years, as some romancers would have us believe. Nero was killed on the 9th of June 68, so he could not have condemned Paul on the 29th. There was no persecution of the Christians in 65, so Paul could not have suffered then; but in 64, in the month of June, there was, as recorded by Tacitus, the terrible persecution in which Paul and his converts suffered, exactly two years after he came to Rome, agreeing with St. Luke's narrative where he distinctly says Paul dwelt two whole years in Rome.

X.

TRES TABERNÆ: A TOPOGRAPHICAL STUDY.

FROM earliest childhood one has been familiar with the words of St. Luke, as he relates the story of St. Paul's journey to Rome: "And from thence, when the brethren heard of us, they came to meet us as far as Appii Forum, and the Tres Tabernæ" (Acts xxviii. 15).

To the Christian traveller visiting Rome nothing perhaps is more satisfactory than to visit the places hallowed by the memory of the great apostle to the Gentiles, and there, as it were, to follow in his footsteps and draw closer to God through his example. Of the places thus hallowed in the vicinity of Rome those where the apostle was met by the Christian brethren are perhaps most cherished. Of Appii Forum there is no doubt. Its site is well known (43 miles off); but of the site of the Tres Tabernæ there has been considerable confusion. We know that it was situated between the first meeting-place and the city of Paul's martyrdom; and perhaps to identify its exact position is no great matter. Whether we go a long or a short distance along "the queen of long routes," it makes no great difference—we are treading in the footsteps of St. Paul. We know that his feet trod those now rough stones; that he gazed on the same landscape that we do, and that many of the objects now in ruin and decay were then in their freshness and beauty; that he passed along this road, and there is no doubt that he was met by certain of the brethren at two distinct places. The first of these places is well known, never having lost its name; the second has been located at various spots. The majority may be indifferent as to where the exact meeting-place was; but to one whose life is devoted to topographical and archæological pursuits there is a certain satisfaction in rescuing it from the dust of ages, particularly when, as often happens, we can sweep away the cobwebs of false statements and plagiarism and uphold history by the light of modern criticism and research.

It seems that two distinct bands of Christians went out to meet the apostle, and encountered him at two different places. Those going the farthest distance (43 miles) were doubtless his kinsmen and wealthier brethren, who could obtain means and give the time for making the journey. Those who met him at the shorter distance were probably the poorer members of the community, who, after their day's work, could walk out and meet the captive for Christ's sake. All of them uniting at the Tres Tabernæ would there pass the night, and on the morrow make an early start for the city to avoid the heat, for it was in the month of June 62 that the journey was finished.

In order to identify the second meeting-place, it is necessary first to make some quotations from fourth century authors. The name in our New Testament is translated "Three Taverns." It is a very unusual thing to translate the name of a place; and Tres Tabernæ means, not "three taverns" but "three shops." These gave the name to the station.

"When [A.D. 306] the Cæsar Maxentius was made emperor, Severus, now deserted by his [army], fled to Ravenna; for Herculius came hither, having been called by his son Maxentius, and, having deceived Severus by perjury, betrayed him into custody, and led him, dressed as a captive, to the city [Rome], and detained him a prisoner in a state villa at the thirteenth mile on the Appian Way. Afterwards, when Galerius marched into Italy, he was strangled and then brought back to the eighth mile,* and was buried in the tomb of Gallienus" ("Excerpta Valesiana," iv. 10; circa A.D. 385).

"Severus was extinguished near to the Tres Tabernæ of Rome by Herculius Maximianus, and his body was placed in the Sepulchre of Gallienus, which is nine * miles from the city [Rome] on the Appian Way" (Aurelius Victor, "Ep." xl. 3; A.D. 370).

Joseph Scaliger has a true and remarkable criticism on the "Excerpta." He says:—"That villa belonging to the state was three miles from the Taverns; for the opinion of Valesius, that Tres Tabernæ was thirty miles distant from Rome, is false [mistaken], because by the consent of all [authorities] the tabula [map] is vicious [full of faults, corrupt] on which he relied between Bovillæ and Ariccia" ("Ad Eusebium," *M.* MMCCCXXIII.).

The Villa Sta. Caterina is just thirteen miles, or two beyond the Tres Tabernæ. If it was three miles, as Scaliger supposes, it was most probably the Villa of Domitian and formerly of Pompey the Great, now covered by the town of Albano.

* Eight miles from the Porta Appia, but nine miles from the Porta Capena.

"Herculius Maximianus persuaded Severus to come to Rome, having promised by a sacred oath that he would protect him. But when Severus, on his road to Rome, had arrived at a certain place, which is called the Tres Tabernæ, he was suddenly taken by those whom Maximianus had placed in ambush, and murdered by being strangled" (Zosimus, ii. 10; A.D. 410).

The Tres Tabernæ here mentioned was on the Via Flaminia, three miles from Terni (Interamna), at a place now called Ponteconfino. (See Rupertus and Cluverus, "Italica Antiqua," iii. 8.)

It appears that he was taken at Tres Tabernæ, north of Rome, then led through the city to the villa near Tres Tabernæ on the Via Appia, where he was finally murdered, when Galerius marched towards Rome. The "Jerusalem Itinerary" gives Mutatio Tribus Tabernis MIII. from Interamna.

"Galerius Augustus had sent Severus Cæsar with an army towards Rome against Maxentius. Whilst Severus was besieging the city, he was betrayed and abandoned by his soldiers, and having therefore taken to flight, he was murdered at Ravenna" (Paulus Orosius, vii. 28).

"Severus Cæsar was sent to Rome by Galerius Maximian in order to seize Maxentius; but his own soldiers having betrayed him, he was slain" (Socrates, "E. H.," i. 2; A.D. 440).

"Severus, taking flight from Ravenna, was killed" (Eutropius, x. 3; A.D. 364).

"He fled to Ravenna, where he shut himself up with a few soldiers; and when he foresaw that he would be betrayed to Maximianus, he gave himself up, and resigned the purple robe to [Galerius from] whom he had received it. In so doing he gained nothing but a good death; for having opened his veins, [he] is compelled to die gently. After that [murder] he [Maximianus] began to persecute his party" (Lactantius, "De Mortibus Persecutorum," xxvi.; A.D. 330).

"Then Galerius came with very great forces towards Rome, threatening the state with ruin, and encamped at Interamna [Terni] on the Tiber" ("Excerpta Valesiana," iii. 6).

The above authors agree that he was betrayed and killed, and then Galerius came; but they are not very clear in their story, and Lactantius differs as to the mode of death. We quote them notwithstanding, as they bear on the subject under discussion.

The "Excerpta Valesiana" says he was kept a prisoner in a villa belonging to the state at the thirteenth mile on the Appian Way, and there strangled.

Aurelius Victor says it was near to the Tres Tabernæ; and both agree that he was buried in the tomb of Gallienus, the "Excerpta" saying "brought back to," making the information stronger—that is to say, from the villa at the thirteenth mile where he was murdered the body was brought back towards Rome to the ninth mile.

Zosimus informs us that the place where Severus was arrested was on the road between Ravenna and Rome at the Tres Tabernæ of the Flaminian Way, and which must not be confounded with the place of the same name on the Appian Way (Tres Tabernæ on the Flaminian Way is seventy-three miles from Rome) near which Severus was murdered, as is done by Zosimus, who writes as though the death immediately followed the arrest. He evidently did not know that there were more than one Tres Tabernæ.

But an older and perhaps more certain authority furnishes us with the exact topographical site of the Tres Tabernæ. We refer to the great orator Marcus Tullius Cicero, who mentions the Tres Tabernæ in his letters.

"But see how strange! I had comfortably come out of the Antian Way into the Appian Way at the Tres Tabernæ, on the festival of Ceres, when my Curio, coming from Rome, met me. At the same place came your servant with letters from you [from Tusculum]......I have written this letter at the tenth hour [4 p.m.] on April 12th [B.C. 58]" (Cicero, "Ad Atticum," ii. 10 [12]).

"Therefore I shall expect you then at Formiæ until the 7th of May. Now, let me know on what day I shall see thee. From Appii Forum at the fourth hour [10 P.M.]. I wrote a little while before from the Tres Tabernæ" (*Ibid.*, ii. 11 [10]).

"Could worse have happened—that is to say, that to your sweetest of epistles no one should have delivered you my answer written at the Tres Tabernæ?" (*Ibid.*, ii. 13.)

The Antian Way (still in use) runs out of the Via Appia at the eleventh mile. Here join the four roads—the Via Appia, the Via Appia Nova, the road to the Via Latina, and the Via Antia. In the ancient days the four roads to Rome from Aricia, Antium, Alba Longa, and Tusculum met here. Thus of necessity there would be a station or halting-place at the meeting of the roads; so here, at this meeting of the roads, on the authority of Cicero, we must fix the site of the Tres Tabernæ: "The Antian leads into the Appian Way at the Tres Tabernæ." This is confirmed by Aurelius Victor and the "Excerpta Valesiana." The spot is now called Frattocchie. Cicero wrote the first letter we have quoted, he tells us, at the tenth hour—

that is, 4 P.M. He continues his journey, and writes the second letter, he says, at the fourth hour—that is, the fourth hour of the night (10 P.M.). So it took him six hours to do the distance between the Tres Tabernæ and Appii Forum (*thirty-two miles*) and write to Atticus.

Often travelling between Rome and Antium, Cicero would be familiar with the Tres Tabernæ, and his local knowledge would be of service, five years after he had written from there to Atticus, when he composed his speech in defence of Milo, for this was the scene of the death of Publius Clodius. Milo was going to Lanuvium on the 20th of January. He left Rome after attending the senate about 3 P.M., and was passing by the Villa of Clodius, the grounds of which skirted the road, at 5 P.M., when he was attacked by Clodius. In the fight which took place Clodius was wounded in front of the shrine of the Bona Dea, which is in the farm of Titus Sextus Gallius, and carried into the neighbouring tavern. Milo ordered him to be dragged out, and he was slain. The body was left there all night, and brought into Rome next day by Sextus Tedius and burned in the Senate House, which was destroyed in the fire which ensued (Cicero and Asconius).

The testimonies we have quoted show conclusively that the Tres Tabernæ of the Appian Way was at the eleventh mile from Rome; that the Colonna farm occupied the site of the farm of Gallius; and that the place is now called Frattocchie, where shops still exist, a tavern, a wheelwright's, a church, and the farm-house of the Colonnas.

Horace, in his celebrated journey, does not mention the Tres Tabernæ, because he broke his journey at Aricia, thence he proceeded to Appii Forum, "filled with sailors and surly landlords" ("Sat." i. 5-7), forty-three miles from Rome. He says good travellers made the distance in one journey.

Before closing our quotations we must cite two modern authors. First, the late Mr. Pentland, who thoroughly explored the Roman Campagna, and the author of "Murray's Handbook to Rome." He says:—"Exactly corresponding with the site of the ninth mile, and on the right side of the Via Appia, is a considerable ruin, supposed to be the tomb of Gallienus, and in which at a later period was buried the Emperor Alexander Severus [the Cæsar Flavius Valerius Severus], who died at the neighbouring mutatio or halting-place of the Tres Tabernæ. The mass of walls behind marks the site of the Villa of Gallienus, which we know from Aurelius Victor was here. This site was excavated during the last century by Gavin Hamilton, an English artist settled at Rome, when the Discobolus, now in the Museum of the Vatican, and several other good specimens of ancient sculpture were discovered. The Roman station Ad Nonum, or Tres Tabernæ, was close to this spot" (Murray's "Rome." 1870).

Our second quotation is from the late Rev. Dr. H. Philip, well known as a missionary to the Jews in Rome for many years. In his illustrated pamphlet on Appii Forum and the Three Taverns he considers them as one locality, and places them at the eighth mile on the Via Appia at the Temple of Hercules. He also gives another opinion, that of the Roman Jews: "About one mile further on is an indistinct ruin, not far from a larger ruin which is pointed out as the tomb of Gallienus, which is called Tres Tabernæ."

We make these two quotations in fairness to show that the idea of the Tres Tabernæ being *near* to Rome, as Aurelius Victor says, was not quite lost.

Now, on the other hand, what have we to array against this mass and weight of evidence? Virtually nothing of authority, but a good deal on paper. The numerous British authors who have written on the travels of St. Paul (we cannot say gone over the ground), and foreigners who have followed in their prints, place the Tres Tabernæ in the Pontine Marshes. Even they are not agreed as to the site or distance from Rome. The oldest of these writers is Eustace (1802), who says, "The village of Cisterna, *probably* on the site of the Tres Tabernæ, is lively and pleasing" ("Classical Tour," xxi.). Cisterna is thirty miles from Rome. Riechard (1820) says, "At Cisterna the traveller crosses the Astura. *Some antiquaries pretend* that this was the place mentioned by St. Luke in the Acts of the Apostles under the name of Tres Tabernæ. Others suppose that the ruins of it may be seen at Sermoneta, about eight miles from Cisterna, to which there is a post road to Velletri" ("Itinerary of Italy").

Sir William Gell (1846) says "the Mutatio ad Tres Tabernas was seven miles from Ariccia, or twenty-three from Rome. The mutatio, however, was not exactly at the twenty-third mile. Its distance exceeded twenty-three miles, but not twenty-four complete" ("Topography of Rome"). In other words, he locates it near Civitone. Now follow Farrar, Conybeare and Howson, M'Leod, Macduff,[*] Merivale, Rénan, and his copyist Labanca. They all copy from one another *without acknowledgment*, and whatever authority they may be on theology they are certainly none on topography.

Rénan states that the site of Appii Forum is now S. Donato. In this he is copied by Baldassare Labanca without acknowledgment.

---

[*] We heard these sermons preached, and this author frankly says that he never visited the places.

Now Appii Forum has never lost its name; to this day it is called Foro Appio. S. Donato is not on the Via Appia, but four miles to the south-west beyond Appii Forum.

We do not believe that any one of these later authors has ever been over the ground, or they would have known that Cisterna *is not on the line* of the ancient Via Appia; that this place, called in the middle ages Cisterna Neronis, is the ancient Ulubræ (Horace, "Ep.," i. 11), whose inhabitants Cicero ("Ad Fam.," iii. 11) calls frogs, and it is to the right of the Via Appia going from Rome. Piale's map marks Tres Tabernæ as at Cisterna; Sickler, on his map, marks it at Casal delle Castelle, two miles this side of Cisterna. Nibby makes a most unaccountable blunder in speaking of the tomb of Gallienus. He says:—" Secondo Sesto Aurelio Vittore, fu seppellito eziandio Severo Cæsar, morto alla stazione delle Tre Taberne, posta sulla Via Appia, *là dove questa traversava le campagne Pontine*" (where this traverses the Pontine Campagna—" Itinerario di Roma"). Now Aurelius Victor never says anything of the sort. The words which we have italicized are an interpolation of Nibby's. (See quotation from Victor above.)

In the case of Gell's theory being the site, Cicero would have taken six hours to do the twenty miles to Appii Forum; whilst if Cisterna is the site, he would have taken the same time to do thirteen miles, and that on a level road. This does not agree with the Tres Tabernæ being *near to* Rome. You cannot say a place is near when it is twenty-three or thirty miles away.

The next thing to consider are the "Itineraries." These *are supposed to be* of the end of the fourth century A.D., and are *presumed* to give *the correct distance* from one point to another. Now any one who has studied and collated any part of them knows that they are full of errors and not to be relied upon. We believe them to be of a much later date than that century, and that they are the originators of the errors as to the site of the Tres Tabernæ.

"Vetera Romanorum Itineraria," Petro Wesselingo (Amsterdam, 1735); "Casanatense" (Minerva Library, B. B. XII., 75); The "Antonini Itinerarium," edited by Tobler (S. Gall, 1863).

Iter ab Urbe Appia Via recto itinere ad columnam M. P. CCCCL, 5.
    Aricia, mill. pass. XVI.; thousand paces from Rome.
      Tribus Tabernis XVII.; 33 miles from Rome.
        Appii Forum X.; 43 miles from Rome.
          Terracina XVII.; 61 miles from Rome. [It is 75.]

The mistakes here show that it is not to be relied upon.

TRES TABERNÆ: A TOPOGRAPHICAL STUDY. 77

The Roman passus equalled 5 Roman feet; 1 foot Roman equalled 11.64 inches.
The English mile is 1760 yards = 5280 feet.
The Roman mile is 1000 passus = 4850 feet English.

It is therefore shorter by 430 feet English, or 143⅓ yards.
The "Itinerarium Hieroslymitanum" or "Burdigalense" gives the places in the reverse way—that is, coming towards Rome.

Mutatio ad Medias	M. X.
Civitas Terracina	M. XIII.
Mutatio Appio Foro	M. IX.
Mutatis Sponsas	M. VII.; 37 miles from Rome, or 4 miles beyond Tribus Tabernis of the above.
Civitas Ariccia et Albona	M. XIV.
Mutatio ad Nono	M. VII.
In Urbe Rome	M. IX.; makes it 46 from Terracina to Rome. [It is 75.]

We call attention to the fact that this "Itinerary" makes no mention of the Tres Tabernæ, but gives Mutatis Sponsas fourteen miles from Ariccia, whereas the "Antonini" gives seventeen from Ariccia to Tres Tabernæ. On the whole, this "Itinerary" seems more reliable than the other, and does not mention the Tres Tabernæ between Appii Forum and Ariccia, because there was no such place.

The next is an "Itineraria Picta," or chart route. It represents by straight lines and edifices of various sizes and medallions the roads and towns of the whole Roman world. The original is in the Vienna Library, and is known as the "Tabula Peutingeriana," because *discovered* by Conrad Peutinger in 1525. It *is supposed* to be of the time of Theodosius (335-395).

Putting it into the "Itinerary" form, it would read,—

Bobellas mill. pass. X.	[If he means Bovillæ, it is 11½ miles.]
Ariccia	III. [It is 15½ miles from Rome, not 13.
Sub Lanubio	It is nearly 5 miles from Bovillæ
Tres Tabernas	to Ariccia.]
Terracina	

We have found this tabula useless as a guide to the Campagna. It is full of errors. The compiler could never have gone over the ground. (See sheet 5.) He makes no road from Antium to the Tres Tabernæ—the Via Antia. He omits altogether the town of Appii Forum, which Pliny (iii. 9) mentions in his list of colonies, showing that it was of some importance. He places Terracina, which is upon the sea, inland; and makes a road from it to join his Via Laurentium at a place marked Ad Turres XI., and continues this road to Cuma.

The conclusion of the whole matter is that this chart *discovered* by Peutinger is, on the face of it, a palpable forgery—that is to say, it is medieval, not ancient. The characters used are not ancient, nor is the style of the medallions ancient, whilst the spelling and the whole get up are decidedly very late. The words are written in Gothic characters, whilst the style of the medallions is decidedly medieval. It was first edited by Scheyb, and printed in Vienna in 1753, and copies can be seen at the Victor Emanuele Library (255, 4 e 6) and at the Casanatense, Minerva Library (M. 17 in CC), entitled "Peutingeriana Tabula Itineraria, quæ in Augusta Bibliotheca Vindobonensi" (Vindobonæ, 1753). Another edition is entitled "Theodosiana et Peutingeriana" (R. 116 in CC), and was published by Cherubini Æsci in Piceno (1819). A new edition of Scheyb's was edited by Conrad Manerti, and published by Hahn in Lipsiæ in 1824, containing twelve plates and costing thirty-six francs. A late edition is that of Earnest Desjardins (Paris: Hachette, 1869. Vittorio Emanuele Library, 102 Scaff Medio 3). A new edition has been published by Dr. Konrad Miller (Ravensburg, 1888) in the original colours, and can be purchased for a few shillings. This is the tabula which Scaliger says "is full of faults," and which we pronounce to be a forgery. It actually shows the towns of Pompeii and Herculaneum, which were destroyed and buried in 79.

We have thus demonstrated to the unbiassed mind that the Tres Tabernæ of the Via Appia, where the Christian brethren met St. Paul, was eleven Roman miles out from the Porta Capena of Rome, or nine English miles three hundred and twenty-six yards from the Porta Appia, at the junction of the Via Appia Antica with the Via Appia Nova, at the farm of the Colonnas, by the tavern of Frattocchie, just over nine English miles from the Porta S. Sebastiano.

The passages in the "Excerpta Valesiana" and in Zosimus led us to go carefully into the whole matter of the site of the Tres Tabernæ, and to examine the ground. The result we have demonstrated above, and have thus rescued another historical site from oblivion.

APPENDIX.

IT will be noticed that the Acts of the Apostles, as also the Second Epistle to Timothy, terminate in a very abrupt manner, which some important crisis must have caused. St. Luke, after saying that Paul dwelt in Rome two years, which period agrees with Nero's persecution, ends his narrative; and doubtless, as he had attached himself to St. Paul in life, so he ended his days with the same firmness, and they, in all probability, perished together. Timothy is supposed by some to have answered the earnest appeal of St. Paul, and to have come to Rome and suffered soon after his father in the Lord. His body is said to be interred in St. Paul's. St. Mark escaped the persecution, and carried the news of Paul's death to Peter and the churches in Asia. The family of Pudens and Clement likewise escaped the cruelty of Nero and the Romans, to carry on the apostle's work. Aquila and Priscilla were absent from Rome at the time. Linus became the first bishop of the church in Rome; so, by a curious coincidence, the first bishop of the Roman Church, and the first Christian emperor of Rome, Constantine, were both members of the British royal family.

Termination of St Luke's narrative.

Dispersion.

There is no authority whatever for the story of the Roman Catholic Church that St. Paul was martyred at a place called the Three Fountains, about three miles outside the Ostian Gate (now Porta San Paolo), off from the main road; and the ridiculous stories told of his head touching the earth three times, and at each bound a fountain springing up, of his saying good-bye to St. Peter (the pretended site is fixed by a little chapel), and of Plautilla and the handkerchief, are all pious frauds, like many other stories in Rome, which will not bear the light of modern criticism.

Pious frauds.

APPENDIX.

House of Nero. The Golden House of Nero was not built till after the death of St. Paul, so he could not have seen the building of which we have the ruins.

Mamertine Prison. There is no evidence whatever to show that St. Paul was confined in the Mamertine Prison. He was condemned to death, not imprisonment; and certainly not in the lower chamber where the fountain is. That spring existed in the days of Jugurtha, before Paul's time, and the chamber was used for those condemned to death by starvation or by strangulation, and not for simple imprisonment.

Body. Part of St. Paul's body is said to exist in St. Peter's, part in St. Paul's outside the walls, his head at the Lateran, an arm at S. Paolo alla Regola, a finger at S. Spirito, and teeth are in various other churches. If so, he has been divided up pretty thoroughly. These are other pious frauds probably. The historian Guicciardini says that when Rome was sacked by the Imperialists (1527) they took the bodies of Peter and Paul, which were then in St. Peter's, and after dragging them about the streets, the remains were thrown into the Tiber. However, relics are exhibited in St. Peter's which are said to be those of both the apostles.

Skit of Crucifixion. In the course of excavating on the Palatine Hill, in one part of the palace, called the Gelotianus, which was the quarters of the soldiers and servants, there was found scratched on the plaster of the second century wall of a small room a caricature of the crucifixion—a man with a donkey's head being crucified, whilst another man is looking at it. Underneath is written in Greek letters—"Alexamenos adores his God." It is of the time of Septimius Severus.

Tertullian ("Apol.," xvi.) tells us that this was a common skit against the Christians, and we would account for it in this way. The Romans mixed up the Christians and the Jews. They had an idea that the Jews worshipped a white donkey (Tacitus, "Hist.," v. 3, 4), and understanding that the Christian's God was crucified, *Reply.* they thus made fun of a Christian soldier, and his reply was found scratched beneath it—"Alexamenos is faithful." See "Rambles in Rome," seventh edition, page 10.

Perhaps the finest monument ever erected in this world is the

APPENDIX.

church at Rome to the memory of St. Paul—St. Paul's outside the walls. The original building, founded in the time of Constantine, was destroyed by fire in 1823; and the present edifice—one vast hall of marbles and mosaics—has been reared by contributions given by the whole world. A Christian lady named Lucina (supposed to be Pomponia Græcina) concealed the body of St. Paul after his martyrdom at her villa on the Via Ostiensis. After a short interval she removed it to a crypt in her farm on the Appian Way. In 254 or 258 the body was removed by another Lucina (the name means a Lady of Light) to its present resting-place, above which the church was founded by Constantine. Beneath the high altar is a small crypt, seven feet long by four feet wide; the floor is composed of four pieces of white marble (*see cover of this work*), one piece occupying the whole length of the crypt. Above it is a slab a trifle smaller, the difference being made up by two pieces at the top left-hand end. It has inscribed upon it in two lines, in characters of the time of Constantine,—

Memorial.

The Tomb of St. Paul.

PAVLO
APOSTOLO MART.

It faces towards the apse of the church, which was the original entry into the basilica when founded by Constantine. Between the two lines, under the A in Paulo, is a circular hole six inches in diameter, once closed with a bronze cover, into which a censer-pot (thurible) fitted. Cutting through the top and bottom of the letters V and L of the name are two square holes, one above the other, to the right and above the circular opening. These square holes are not original. At the base of the first, which is seven inches square, a passage leads into the second hole, six by six and three-quarter inches; and from the second hole another passage leads into the round hole. These square holes were for the priests to put in objects which the pilgrims might desire to come in contact, as near as possible, with the martyr. The floor of this crypt is the level of the floor of the original church—that is to say, the memorial marble slab formed part of the original floor; and it has every appearance of never having been disturbed since it was placed there in the time of Constantine.

Prudentius ("Passio Beat. Apost.") describes the original memorial, and his words are just as applicable to the present edifice:—

> "Imperial splendour all the roof adorns;
> Whose vaults a monarch built to God, and graced
> With golden pomp the vast circumference.

> With gold the beams he covered, that within
> The light might emulate the beams of morn.
> Beneath the glittering ceiling pillars stood
> Of Parian stone, in fourfold ranks disposed;
> Each curving arch with glass of various dye
> Was decked: so shines with flowers the painted mead
> In spring's prolific day."

The Platonia on the Appian Way. A passage from the Church of S. Sebastian gives access to the original resting-place of St. Paul, which has recently been cleared out, and is now open to visitors. Anastasius records that Damasus in 366 built and adorned the chapel, where the bodies of the apostles were laid. It was called Platonia, because it was decorated with marble. He also records its restoration by Adrian I., 772-95. It is a large apse in shape, the original entry being in the straight side. The outer wall of the front, formerly a portico, is decorated with eleventh-century frescoes of Christ in an aureole supported by two angels, with portraits of St. Peter and St. Paul on the sides, the Massacre of the Innocents, the Madonna enthroned with two angels and four prophets—beneath which are portraits of SS. Fabianus and Sebastian with two angels—and the Crucifixion. Some of the original floor in black and white mosaic still exists, and part of a thirteenth-century copy of the inscription of Damasus, which is handed down to us in the Einsiedeln MSS. of the eighth century:—

> "You should know that here saints once dwelt.
> Whoever asks for their names, Peter and Paul together.
> Disciples, sent from the east, which we freely acknowledge.
> For their blood's merit they followed Christ to the stars,
> And sought the inner heaven, and the kingdom of bliss.
> Rome rather defends her meriting citizens.
> Damasus relates thus your praise, O new stars."

In the centre of the Platonia, beneath the altar, is the crypt where the bodies rested, that of St. Peter having been, according to tradition, placed here by Calixtus I. in 220, when Elagabalus pulled down part of Nero's circus. His body was removed to the Vatican in 258 by Sixtus II. "Tertio Kalendas Julias, Tusco et Basso consulibus, Pietro in Vaticano, Paulo in Via Ostiensis utriusque in catacumbas."—*Bucherianum Calendar.* Anastasius says it was Cornelius who removed the bodies in 254. Probably the little chapel half way between the Porta S. Paolo and his basilica marks the spot where the bodies were parted. Upon the altar are seventeenth-century busts of the apostles, and on each side Gothic windows, by which objects could be placed on the temporary resting-place of the apostles by the pilgrims. Thirteen *arcosolia* recesses, once the resting-places of early bishops of Rome, are formed in the curve of the apse, and still bear traces of beautiful stucco and fresco work.

Off the west corner of the Palatine Hill stands the archaic altar erected at the end of the Via Nova to appease the unknown deity whose warning voice they had neglected to obey when the Gauls captured Rome in B.C. 390. Livy, Cicero, Juvenal, Plutarch, Aulus Gellius, and Varro all write about it. It is not *in situ*, being placed here when found. Originally it stood farther up, " where the Via Nova turned into the Velabrum." The inscription reads :—

The Altar to the Unknown Deity.

```
SEI DEO SEI DEIVAE SAC
C SEXTIVS C T CALVINVS PR
DE SENATI SENTENTIA RESTITVIT.
```

C. Sextius Calvinus was consul in B.C. 124, and his son was prætor in B.C. 99 (Cicero, "Brutus," xxxiv. 130; "De Orat." ii. 61), when he restored the altar. It naturally reminds us of the similar altar which St. Paul saw on Mars Hill, and which he used as a text when preaching to the Athenians. That altar was doubtless erected to the deity who caused earthquakes, the personality of whom was unknown to the ancients. So Greeks and Romans, when in doubt, and to avoid any unpleasantness if they erected the altar to either a god or goddess, dedicated it to the one or the other. This altar St. Paul must likewise have seen when he visited the palace of the Cæsars.

The apostle tells us that the Word was heard throughout the Prætorian camp, and that he had converts amongst the household of Nero. At first sight it seems difficult to understand how St. Paul, a prisoner, could have preached to the Prætorians and have saints in the household of the emperor. It was really a natural sequence of events—opportunities that offered, and of which the apostle took advantage. St. Paul was a prisoner to the military authorities, rescued from the Jews by the soldiers, taken by them to Cæsarea, held there, brought to Rome, and consigned to the Prætorians by Julius the centurion, who held him in their custodianship for two years. His guard would be changed, according to military usage, every twenty-four hours, so that he had personal contact with at least 731 different Prætorians during the two years; and thus their prisoner preached to them and their comrades. Now these Prætorians furnished the guard to the Palatine Hill, and, as their prisoner, he had

" So we preach, and so ye believed" (1 Cor. xv. 11).

entry to the palace of the Cæsars, "none forbidding him;" and so he conversed with and made converts ("saints") in Cæsar's household. Thus he obeyed the Lord's command: "So must thou bear witness also at Rome" (Acts xxiii. 11).

WAS ST. PETER EVER IN ROME?

This question is repeatedly asked us, and our reply is that there is no historic evidence for such a supposition, though the Roman Catholic Church contends that he came to Rome in A.D. 42, and was bishop of the church there for twenty-five years—till A.D. 66—when he suffered martyrdom in Nero's Circus.* It may be interesting to our readers to show where Peter was during those years, A.D. 42-66.

It is computed that St. Paul's conversion took place A.D. 37. He says, "Then after three years I went up to Jerusalem to see Peter, and abode with him fifteen days" (Gal. i. 18). This brings us to A.D. 40. After the meeting at Jerusalem "Peter passed throughout all quarters; he came down also to the saints which dwelt at Lydda" (Acts ix. 32). From thence he went to Joppa, and raised Tabitha (ver. 36, 41). "And it came to pass, that he tarried many days in Joppa" (ver. 43). From Joppa he went to Cornelius at Cæsarea. "Then prayed they him to tarry certain days" (Acts x. 48); after which he returned to Jerusalem (Acts xi. 2). These journeys would bring us to the end of the year 42. In A.D. 44, just before Easter, Herod took Peter and put him in prison (Acts xii. 4); but he, being delivered by an angel, "departed, and went into another place" (ver. 17). Paul says, "Then fourteen years after I went up again to Jerusalem" (Gal. ii. 1). This is fourteen years after his conversion, which brings us to A.D. 51, the year of the Council of the Apostles, when "Peter rose up, and spake unto them" (Acts xv. 7). Again, Paul says Peter came to Antioch (Gal. ii. 11), where Paul rebuked him. Socrates, the ecclesiastical historian (vi. 8), says Peter was bishop of Antioch, so he could not have been bishop of Rome also.

After this event no further mention is made of Peter in the Acts; but St. John records (ch. xxi. 18, 19) these words of Jesus concerning Peter: "When thou shalt be old, thou shalt stretch forth thy hands, and another shall gird thee, and carry thee whither thou wouldest

* Three places are pointed out as the scene of his martyrdom—St. Pietro in Montorio on the Janiculum, the Prati Cosimato, and Nero's Circus. If he suffered in Rome, it was doubtless in Nero's Circus.

not. This spake he, signifying by what death he should glorify God." This was pointing to St. Peter's martyrdom, and the words of our Lord imply rather that Peter had his eyes put out before he finally suffered, than that he was crucified, but where or when we have no trustworthy account. It was certainly after Paul's death; for Peter's epistle, carried by Paul's companion Silas or Silvanus, "to the strangers scattered throughout Pontus, Galatia, Cappadocia, Asia, and Bithynia"—churches founded by Paul, and under his mission—would not have been written by him if Paul had been still living. He says, "The things which are now reported unto you by them that have preached the gospel unto you" (1 Peter i. 12). This was written from Babylon, A.D. 65; and in ch. v. 13 he speaks of Mark as being with him. He must, therefore, have carried the news of St. Paul's death to Peter; for in Paul's Epistle to Philemon, just before his death (A.D. 64), we have Mark mentioned as his fellow-labourer, and in Colossians iv. 10 Mark is spoken of as coming unto them. In Peter's first epistle (iv. 17), he says, "For the time is come that judgment must begin at the house of God." Peter's second epistle (A.D. 66) is addressed to the same churches; and in ch. iii. 15, 16, he says, "Even as our beloved brother Paul also according to the wisdom given unto him hath written unto you; as also in all his epistles, speaking in them of these things." He evidently refers to the death of Paul, which happened in the persecution under Nero, A.D. 64; and it was evidently written shortly before his own death, probably A.D. 66, for in ch. i. 14 he says, "Knowing that shortly I must put off this my tabernacle, even as our Lord Jesus Christ hath shewed me."

We left Peter at Antioch in A.D. 51, not having as yet visited Rome, and from St. Paul's writings it is clear that up to his death Peter had not arrived; and after his death we have Peter writing to the churches of Paul's foundation from Babylon. Paul, writing to the Romans, A.D. 58 (ch. i. 11), says, "For I long to see you, that I may impart unto you some spiritual gift, to the end ye may be established." That is the church founded by Aquila and Priscilla in their house. And again: "I am ready to preach the gospel to you that are at Rome also" (ver. 15). "So have I strived to preach the gospel, not where Christ was named, lest I should build upon another man's foundation" (ch. xv. 20). And writing to the Galatians (ch. ii. 7): "The gospel of the uncircumcision was committed unto me, as the gospel of the circumcision was unto Peter." It is evident from these passages that up to this date Peter had not been in Rome, where Paul arrived A.D. 62, when he called the chief of the Jews together (Acts xxviii. 17), and they said, "For as concerning this sect, we know that everywhere it is spoken against" (ver. 22). This also shows that Peter could not have preached in Rome; and during Paul's residence in his own hired house, though he writes many epistles containing salutations from the church at Rome, and mentions names of its members, Peter is not mentioned. And at the last, A.D. 64, just before his death, he says, "Only Luke is with me" (2 Tim. iv. 11). This he would not have said if Peter had been with him; in fact they do not seem to have met after Paul withstood him to the face. Peter's epistles, dated from Babylon, give us the key of the fable of his coming to Rome; for St. John in the Revelation (A.D. 69) refers to Rome under the symbolic name of Babylon. Hence in the third century the story began to gain ground that Peter wrote from Rome itself, till in the fourth it is mentioned in the works of the fathers, who do not agree with each other either as to the time of his coming or the length of his stay.

The Roman Church has mixed up a local St. Peter and a St. Paul who were put to death under Gallienus, A.D. 260, whose *festa* is October 3rd, and this has led to the idea that both of the apostles were together in Rome and suffered on the same day.

THE CHRISTIAN EMPEROR.

Three hundred years after the establishment of the Roman empire under Augustus, occurred that great crisis in Roman history which rent the empire, established a new religion, and led to the fall of Rome. From "the isles afar off" came the shrewd politician and consummate general Constantine the Great, the British emperor, around whose life so many romantic stories and fanciful episodes are woven. This man, inheriting a part of the Roman empire, desired the rest, determining to be master alone; and casting about for ways and means, did not fail to observe that there existed, permeating through all ranks of society, a new religious feeling that was contrary to and utterly irreconcilable with any of the religious forms that had served the old Roman mind for upwards of a thousand years. The cause of this new religion gave him the excuse to gratify his ambition. He made friends with and protected the Christians in his part of the empire, for his sagacity showed him that they could be made the stepping-stones to command the world. Later on he saw that the rising religion was the spiritual power of the future, and he tried to combine the two, and to a certain extent was looked upon for a time as the head of the Christian Church.

These few remarks may perchance direct the thoughts of our and his fellow-countrymen to the life of this extraordinary man, which may be appropriately studied amidst the ruins of that seat of empire which he despoiled. As his origin and birthplace seem to be surrounded with some obscurity, we will endeavour to throw light on the subject.

Eutropius (x. 2) tells us: "Constantius Chlorus died at York, after being emperor thirteen years. He was succeeded by Constantine, his son by a wife of obscure birth." "Constantius is said to have been the grand-nephew of Claudius by a daughter" (Eutropius, ix. 22).

Zosimus (i. 2) says: "Constantine was declared emperor in Britain on the death of his father." And Polydore Vergil ("Historia Britannia," page 381) records that "Constantine, born in Britain, of a British mother, proclaimed emperor in Britain, beyond doubt made his natal soil a participator in his glory."

Sozomen ("E. H.," i. 5) says: "The Great Constantine received his Christian education in Britain."

From the above passages there is no doubt that Constantine was born and declared emperor in England; but who was his mother? Eutropius says she was of obscure birth. To this Greek her birth may have seemed obscure, as he knew nothing of her native land. He was secretary to Constantine, and ought as an historian to have informed himself. Let us now see if we can find any authority for fixing the social position of the celebrated Empress Helena, the mother of Constantine, and first wife of Constantius Chlorus.

Trebellius Pollio, in his "Life of Claudius" (xiii.), says: "Flavius Constantius Chlorus was the son of Eutropius, one of the great lords of Dardania (a portion of Moesia Superior), and of Claudia, daughter of Crispus, brother to the Emperor Claudius the Goth." "Before the title of Cæsar was conferred on him (by Diocletian in 293) he married Helena; but he was forced to divorce her, conformable to the will of Hercules Maximianus and Diocletian, who obliged him to marry Theodora, the daughter of Hercules and Eutropia" (Aurelius Victor). "Helena was unquestionably a British princess," says Melancthon ("Ep.," page 189).

This last author gives her the title of princess, which is confirmed by other writers.

Camden says: "Constantius married Helena, daughter of Coilus, who entertained him when he was the governor of Britain. But Maximianus declared Constantius Cæsar, on condition he would forsake Helena and marry Theodora."

"S. Helena is generally considered to have been a British princess, the daughter of King Coilus, and was born either at York or Colchester" (Green, "Saints and their Symbols"). The venerable Archbishop W. B. Ady, in his address from the clergy at Colchester to the Royal Archæological Institute in August 1876, says: "We welcome your coming to our ancient borough, which has a history ranging beyond the present era, and which boasts to be the birthplace of the first Christian emperor, Constantine, the son of a Colchester mother, Helena."

Constantine's panegyrist Eumenius says he was born in Britain: "Britannias illic oriundo nobiles fecisti." Pope Urban in his Brief "Britannia" says: "Christ showed to Constantine the Briton the victory of the cross for his sceptre." Thus we have Helena established as a British princess, the daughter of Cole, King of Colchester, or, as the Romans called it, Camulodunum. As a boy, rambling amidst the Roman and Norman ruins of Colchester, the name of Helena and her chapel were familiar to us. And her cross, in the borough arms with the three crowns, was always in sight. King Coel's Gate, King Coel's Kitchen, and King Coel's Hump, were favourite places and household names, whilst we often sung the words of the local popular song,—

'Old King Cole was a merry old soul.'"

From the "Annals of England" we have compiled the following genealogical table, which makes the subject clear:—

CARADOC-CARACTACUS, Prince of Siluria, A.D. 40-80. Prisoner in Rome, 52; returned to Britain a Christian in 58. First Christian king.

HIS CHILDREN.

GLADYS-CLAUDIA, married in A.D. 53 Aulus Rufus Pudens, the half-brother of St. Paul. Pudens, martyred in 96. Claudia, died in 97. *Their children*—Novatus, died 108; Timotheus, died 140; Pudentiana, died 107; Praxedes, died 140.

CYLLINUS, Coel I., A.D. 120. *His son was*—Lleiver Mawr-St. Lucius, baptized at Winchester by his uncle Timotheus in 139. *His daughter*—Gladys, married Cadvan, Prince of Cambria. *Their daughter*—Strada the fair, married Coel II., King of Colchester, 232. *Their daughter*—Helena, married Julius Constantius Chlorus, Emperor of Rome, 296-306. *Their son, born 276, was afterwards* CONSTANTINE THE GREAT, the first Christian Emperor, 306-337.

LLEY-LINUS, the first bishop of Rome. Martyred A.D. 81.

It is curious that Eusebius—who wrote a "Life of Constantine," and recounts some of the legends evolved round him and Helena—says nothing whatever of the family of Helena, or of the birthplace of Constantine.

Here is another legend, new to us, published in "The Story of St. Helena," 1887, by the St. Helena Home for Nurses, London : "There seems no reason to doubt also that Helena was a British princess, daughter of the governor of Cornwall, and was born at Carnarvon, or as it was then called under the Roman occupation, Segontium. Local tradition still speaks of her; and the use of her name to designate Helen's Well, Helen's Causeway, and Helen's Wood, sufficiently attests her connection with the spot."

To all this testimony we must add that of the learned Cardinal Baronius, Vatican librarian, who died in 1607. His language is firm and to the point: "The man must be mad who, in the face of universal antiquity, refuses to believe that Constantine and his mother were Britons, born in Britain" ("Annals," 306).

Notwithstanding this strong array of evidence of the fact that Helena and Constantine were of the British royal family, another opinion has been held. After diligent study and research we are forced to reject it as false, but we append it, so that our readers may see both sides of the question, and take it for what it is worth.

Maunder says : "The mother of Constantine was of obscure birth in Bithynia, and was married by Constantius whilst in that country. Her body was conveyed to Rome, and deposited in the tomb of the emperors." The latter assertion is entirely false. There was no general tomb of the emperors in Rome at that late period; and Eusebius in his "Life of Constantine" (47) says, "She was buried in the imperial mausoleum at Constantinople." This statement is confirmed by Socrates ("E. II.," i. 17): "Helena's remains were conveyed to New Rome (Constantinople) and deposited in the imperial sepulchres." Now, as the latter statement of Maunder is proved to be false, we shall presently prove that the first statement is also false. In fact the numerous citations that we have made above prove it to be erroneous, but we will examine this Bithynia story presently.

Notwithstanding the statement of the two historians that she was buried at Constantinople, three sarcophagi in Rome are claimed as hers. Anyway she could not have had four sarcophagi. In the Church of S. Maria di Ara Cœli a red porphyry sarcophagus in the left transept is pointed out as hers. In the Church of S. Croce in Gerusalemme another is shown; whilst in the hall of the Greek Cross in the Vatican Museum is a third one, a large and finely-sculptured red porphyry sarcophagus of some Roman general of the time of the Antonines, having in high relief Roman soldiers bringing in captives, winged Victories, and the busts of Juno and Diana—not what we might expect to find on a Christian woman's tomb, least of all that of Helena's, though it is ascribed to her.

The great English historian remarks: "The place of Constantine's birth, as well as the condition of his mother Helena, have been the subject not only of literary but of national disputes. Notwithstanding the recent tradition which assigns for her father a British king, we are obliged to confess that Helena was the daughter of an innkeeper" (Gibbon, xiv. 1).

"This tradition, unknown to the contemporaries of Constantine, was invented in the darkness of monasteries, was embellished by Geoffrey of Monmouth and the writers of the twelfth century, has been defended by our antiquaries of the last age, and is seriously related in Carte's 'History of England.' He transports, however, the kingdom of Coil, the imaginary father of Helena, from Essex to the wall of Antoninus" (Note 1*b*).

The "Excerpta Valesiana" says he was born at Naissus. This was a town of Mœsia Superior, the modern Servia. This author has evidently mixed up the birthplace of the son with that of the father—Constantius being born at Naissus, in Dardania, off Mœsia Superior; whilst Constantine was born at Camulodunum, in the country of the Trinobantes, Essex, Britain. This mistake doubtless arose from the similarity of the two names.

We have yet another statement to examine. Procopius of Cæsarea, who died about 560, says in his "De Cæsariensis Ædificiis," v. 2: "In Bithynia there is a city named after Helena, the mother of Constantine, in which *they say* that Helena was born, and which in former times was an inconsiderable village. The Emperor Constantine, out of filial duty, gave this place its name and the dignity of a city, but built nothing there on an imperial or magnificent scale, for the place remained in its former condition in respect of its buildings, but merely had the glory of being called a city, and prided itself on being named after Helena, to whom it had given birth." He then records how it was beautified by Justinian. The city here referred to was Drepanum, on the Asiatic side of the Propontus, the Sea of Marmora. Ammianus Marcellinus (xxvi. 8, 1) says: "The town formerly known as Drepanum, but now as Helenopolis."

It was here that Constantine was taken sick just previous to his death (Eusebius, Life, iv. 61). Socrates, who wrote his Ecclesiastical History about 350, says: "Helena, the emperor's mother (from whose name Drepanum, once a village, having been made a city by the emperor, was called Helenopolis), being divinely directed by dreams, went to Jerusalem" (i. 17). Sozomen, his contemporary, says (ii. 2): "Two cities are named after her, one in Bithynia and the other in Palestine."

Although these authors quoted record the changing of the name, none of them say why it was so changed; so far we have nothing to contradict the *they say* of the late writer Procopius. But a writer who flourished just after the days of Constantine gives quite another story, and the true one, as to the change of name. Philostorgius, in his history as epitomized by Photius, says: "Helena, the mother of the emperor, built the city which was called Helenopolis, at the entrance of the Gulf of Nicomedia; and that the reason of her great predilection for the spot was because the body of the martyr Lucian was carried thither by a dolphin after his death by martyrdom." Thus it appears that Constantine had nothing to do with the naming of the town, but it was the work of his mother.

We have thus proved that neither Naissus nor Drepanum was the birthplace of Helena or of Constantine. We have demonstrated that Helena was a native of Colchester; and the probability is that Constantine was also born there, as stated by Archdeacon Ady, or at York. Constantius was born in the time of Gallienus, 254. He was made Cæsar by Diocletian in 293, when he divorced his wife Helena. Constantine reigned thirty-one years, coming to the throne when thirty, so he must have been born in 276, in the reign of Probus, when his father was stationed in Britain (Vopiscus, "Probus," xxii.). In 283-4 Constantius was governor of Dalmatia (Vopiscus, in "Carus," xvi.), and he did not return to Britain till after the death of Allectus in 297, where he was declared emperor in 305.

"This Constantine was the son of Constantius Chlorus, a Roman general, and was born in Britain while his father was in the island. It is said that his mother was a native of Britain" (Curnow's School History).

THE EARLY BRITISH CHURCH.

So much is just now being said about the disestablishment of that part of the Anglican Church which is located in the principality of Wales, that a few words on the Early British Church, represented now by the Anglican Church in Wales, may not be inappropriate. We have already called attention to the fact that the King of Siluria, Caractacus, was converted to Christianity in Rome, and that he returned to Britain in 58 A.D. and introduced the gospel there, thus fulfilling the prophecy of Isaiah xlix. 23, "And kings shall be thy nursing fathers, and their princesses thy nursing mothers." The gospel thus planted in Britain in apostolic times spread from its western coast eastwards. That this religion was introduced independently of the Romans is clear; for Tertullian says, "Regions of Britain never penetrated by the Roman arms have received the religion of Christ" ("Adv. Jud.," 7).

"The mother church of the British Isles is the church in Insula Avalonia, called by the Saxons Glastonbury" (Augustine's Epistle to Gregory). This is confirmed by Bishop Usher. It is a tradition of the Anglican Church in Wales that their Church was founded by Joseph of Arimathæa, who with others left Palestine after the crucifixion of our Lord, and who brought to Britain the Holy Grail. This is admitted by Cardinal Pole, Genebrard, Theodore Martin, Robert Parsons the Jesuit (vi. 15), Sabelliess (Enno, vii. 5), and other writers. It is also a tradition of the Church in Wales that Simon Zelotes was crucified in Britain, which story is confirmed by Dorotheus, bishop of Tyre, the brother of Barnabas. This British Church sent out its missionaries "to preach the gospel to the whole world." From it Beatus founded the Helvetian Church. Mansuelus of Ireland was converted in Britain, and in company with Clement of Gaul founded the churches of Toul, Treves, and Marseilles.

We have already shown how the second son of Caractacus, Linus, was left in Rome when his father returned to England, and that he became the first bishop of Rome. This is confirmed by Irenæus (iii. 1)—"The apostle, having founded and built up the church at Rome, committed the ministry of its supervision to Linus. This is that Linus mentioned by St. Paul in his epistles to Timothy." It is likewise settled by the Roman "Apostolici Constitutiones" (c. 46)— "Linus, the brother of Claudia (wife of Pudens, the half-brother of

St. Paul, and daughter of Caractacus), was the first bishop ordained by Paul; and after the death of Linus, Clement was the second, ordained by Peter." It is said that Eubulus (2 Tim. iv. 21) was the cousin of Claudia. Timotheus, the son of Pudens and Claudia, was evidently so named after the friend, companion, and brother in the faith of St. Paul. Timotheus visited Britain and baptized his nephew, King Lucius, and his nobility at Winchester. Whilst Timotheus was absent in Britain, Hermes, the pastor of the church in the house of Pudens, wrote his "Epistolæ ad Timotheum," giving us many interesting particulars of the family affairs of Pudens, Claudia, and their daughters. Thus St. Lucius, the second Christian king in the world's history, was also a Briton.

Bede gives the following account of the conversion of St. Lucius, but he seems to be mistaken in several of his statements:—

"In the year of our Lord's incarnation 156, Marcus Aurelius Verus, the fourteenth from Augustus,* was made emperor together with his brother, Aurelius Commodus.† In their time, whilst Eleutherius,‡ a holy man, presided over the Roman Church, Lucius, King of the Britons, sent a letter to him, entreating that by his command he might be made a Christian. He soon obtained his pious request; and the Britons preserved the faith which they had received, uncorrupted and entire, in peace and tranquillity, until the time of the Emperor Diocletian" (i. 4).

That Christianity was introduced into Britain in the time of Tiberius is affirmed in Gildas' "History of Britain," and by Joseph of Arimathæa, who brought the Holy Grail, in the Cottonian Manuscripts; and both traditions are confirmed by Baronius, "Ecclesiastical Annals," 35 A.D. That the first church was at Glastonbury in Somersetshire is affirmed by William of Malmesbury (i. 2), and confirmed by Hearne's "Antiquities of Glastonbury."

During the Diocletian persecutions, which were general all over the Roman world, Christians suffered in Britain, St. Alban amongst

---

* Antoninus Pius was fourteenth from Augustus. He reigned from 138 to 161.

† Commodus was adopted by Hadrian in 134, and took the name of Ælius Verus; he died in 136. Then Hadrian adopted Titus Aurellanus, who reigned after him as Antoninus Pius. He adopted Marcus Aurelius and Lucius Verus, who reigned together eleven years (Eutropius), 161 to 172. Marcus Aurelius died in 180.

‡ He was bishop of Rome from 177 to 180 (Eusebius, v. 22). Anicetus (158-169) and Soterus (169-177) were bishops of Rome under Marcus Aurelius and Lucius Verus. Telesphorus (128-139) was the bishop who sent Timotheus into Britain in the time of Antoninus Pius. He was probably sent as knowing the language and from his connection with the British royal family, through his mother Claudia. He returned to Rome, and died 140.

the rest. In 306 we have the British emperor, Constantine, and his mother Helena, whose sympathies were Eastern, towards the cradle of the Christian Church. At the three councils held in this century—at Arles in 314, Sardis in 347, and Ariminum in 359—British bishops were present.

In 449 Christian Britain was overrun by the pagan English, who established themselves in Kent. Then came over the Saxons, and in 519 established the kingdom of West Saxons. Others followed, so that finally seven kingdoms were established in what is now England.

In 597 Gregory I. (the Great) sent over Augustine as a missionary from Rome, and part of pagan England embraced the Roman Catholic faith, following the example of the King of Kent, Æthelbert, whose capital (Canterbury) became the propaganding centre.

The mission work led to no end of trouble in the history of England, and to many false ideas in the family circle. The many know nothing of the ancient British Church. They are taught that Augustine introduced Christianity into England; but the few know that a Christian church, independent of Rome, founded in apostolic times, flourished in Britain. Æthelbert had married Bertha, the daughter of the King of Paris. She could do nothing with her husband, and called in the priests, who settled him and themselves in his country at the same time. After a little Augustine goes prospecting, and actually finds native Christians who had never heard of the bishop of Rome. He was objected to by the Church of Britain. (Bede, History, ii. 2, and Nicholas Trivet, ii. 4.) In 603 the representatives of the British and Roman Churches met at what is called the Oak Conference, and the British Archbishop of St. David's made a strong protest against the proceedings of Augustine. (See Cottonian Manuscripts, British Museum Library.)

Gregory was dead, his successor was dead, but Bishop Boniface III. reigned in their stead. Less than two years he ruled the Roman Church, but within that period he successfully brought the Emperor Phocas to recognize him and his successors under the title of Pope. Now, Augustine wanted the British Church to do as Phocas had done, but was not so successful. The Britons spoke out: "We have nothing to do with Rome, we know nothing of the bishop of Rome in his new character of the Pope; we are the British Church, the archbishop of which is accountable to God alone, having no superior on earth."

Returning to Canterbury, Augustine tried to corrupt the army, but was equally unsuccessful. The Briton was too much for the Roman, who had talked for some time when the soldier asked, "Does

Rome possess all the truth?" "All," replied Augustine. Then said the soldier: "And you say we do; our usages only differ. Now, of two men, if both have all their limbs and senses complete, both are equal. Because the Romans have noses and we have noses, must we either cut off our noses or be Romans? Must all who have noses be subject to the Romans? Why, then, should all who hold the faith be subject to Rome because she holds the faith?" Augustine prudently held his tongue. Blackstone says: "The ancient British Church, by whomsoever planted, was a stranger to the bishop of Rome and all his pretended authorities" (vol. iv., p. 105).

The Romans nevertheless worked hard to gain their ends, and at a synod held at Whitby in 664 their claims for jurisdiction were partly granted, through the influence of the High Church party.

In 673 a synod was held at Hertford, and under Archbishop Theodore of Canterbury the bishops of the heptarchic kingdoms agreed to recognize him as their head.

In 827 Egbert, the King of the West Saxons, made himself master of the whole of England, and for the first time Albion was called England. He made Winchester his capital.

The single throne of the archbishop led to the single throne of the king, and they entered into partnership; hence the union of Church and State.

In 836 Ethelwulf succeeded his father, and he was the first king in England to pay tribute to Rome; hence his portrait in the Vatican.

Notwithstanding all this, a remnant of the British Church still held out amongst the hills and valleys of Wales, but the end was approaching of their independent will and rule.

In 925 there was born, at Glastonbury, Dunstan, who entered the Church and became abbot of his native town and the early Church. He was a man of enterprise and energy, having tendencies towards Rome. He succeeded in uniting the Churches of Britain and Rome. He was rewarded by being made Archbishop of Canterbury—Primate of England and Wales—961. He died in 988.

Thus for nine hundred years have the Churches of England and Wales been amalgamated.

Just as Dunstan was about to consummate his great work, the devil appeared to him one night and tried to prevent the good deed; but

> "St. Dunstan, as the story goes,
> Pulled the devil by the nose
> With red-hot tongs, which made him roar,
> Till he was heard ten miles or more."

96   THE EARLY BRITISH CHURCH.

The English got used to their British archbishop, and the British to being spiritually ruled from Canterbury. So when, in 1282, the other partner in the union looked with longing eyes upon the hills and valleys of Wales, they yielded them and accepted the English Prince of Wales. The English had now paid the debt they owed for the archbishop by giving a prince to Wales, which represented ancient Britain. State as well as Church was now one in South Britain. The influence of Rome was not found to be of advantage, so, after a series of struggles, in 1531 the partners threw off the yoke of the Church of Rome, and from that time the Church in England has been perfectly independent of the Church of Rome. The religious houses established by Rome were suppressed. The partners, king and archbishop, shared the plunder between them.

PHOTOGRAPHS ILLUSTRATING
THE FOOTSTEPS OF ST. PAUL IN ROME.

WE have prepared the following Photographs which illustrate St. Paul's Footsteps in Rome, being taken from places he actually saw, or from their connection with the Early Church in Rome.

These Forty-eight Historical Photographs are sold in Packets separately from the Work, or can be had bound up with the Work, on Application to Dr. RUSSELL FORBES, 76 Via della Croce, Rome.

Price 24 lire the Set of Forty-eight.

LIST OF PHOTOGRAPHS.

1. Paul's Landing-Place at Puteoli,	*Page*	16
2. Map of Route to Rome,		17
3. Boat passing along the Canal,		18
4. Appii Forum,		18
5. Causeway on the Appian Way,		19
6. Tomb of Aruns,		19
7. Tomb of Pompey the Great,		19
8. Tomb of Clodius,		19
9. Three Taverns,		20
10. Tomb of Gallienus and Severus,		21
11. Tomb of Quintus Veranssius,		21
12. Temple of Hercules,		21
13. Tomb of Persius,		22
14. Tomb of the Horatii,		22
15. Tomb of Cotta,		22
16. Tombs of the Curiatii,		24
17. Tomb of Cecilia Metella,		24
18. Ruins of the Arch of Drusus,		26
19. The Arch. From a Coin,		26
20. Columbaria of the Cæsars' Household,		26
21. Inscription of Tryphena,		27
22. Inscription of Tryphosa,		27
23. Porta Capena. From Reliefs,		28
24. Circus Maximus. From a Coin,		30
25. The Vicus Tuscus,		30
26. Ruins of the Forum Romanum,		30
27. The Forum of Augustus,		39
28. Prætorian Camp. From a Coin,		30
29. Ruins of the Prætorian Camp,		30
30. House of St. Paul,		35
31. Altar of the Lares, Vicus Æscletus,		36
32. House of Aquila,		39
33. Fresco of the Oratory of St. Clement,		40
34. Tomb of the Plautii,		44
35. Arch of Claudius. From a Coin,		44
36. Church and Baptistery of Pudens, and Church of Sta. Pudentiana,		47
37. Plan of Domus Pudentis,		48
38. Wall of the Great Hall,		49
39. The Stadium. From a Coin,		54
40. Bust of Nero,		56
41. Basilica on the Palatine Hill,		60
42. A Silent Witness,		62
43. Junction of the Antian and Appian Ways at the Three Taverns,		73
44. Skit of the Crucifixion,		80
45. St. Paul's Church,		81
46. The Tomb of St. Paul,		81
47. Altar to the Unknown Deity,		83
48. Constantine, the Christian Emperor,		86

WHAT TO READ!

Dr. RUSSELL FORBES'S PUBLICATIONS.

RAMBLES IN ROME. 12mo, limp cloth. Illustrated with Maps and Plans. The best and cheapest Guide-Book on Rome down to date. *Price 6 lire. Seventh Edition.*

THE FOOTSTEPS OF ST. PAUL IN ROME. 12mo, limp cloth. Illustrated. It is as true an account as probably will be written of St. Paul's stay in Rome. *Price 3 lire. Fourth Edition.*

FORTY-EIGHT PHOTOGRAPHS illustrating the above, all connected with St. Paul. *Price lire 24 the Set.*

The work Bound in Roman vellum, and illustrated with 48 photographs. *Price 36 lire.*

RAMBLES IN NAPLES AND ITS NEIGHBOURHOOD. 12mo, limp cloth. Illustrated, and with Maps and Plans. An excellent practical Guide up to date. *Price lire 3.50. Fourth Edition.*

THE FORUM RESTORED. A large Photograph of Dr. Forbes's interesting Discovery of the Forum depicted on Ancient Reliefs. With Descriptive Letterpress. *Price 1 lira.*

THE MUSEUMS OF ROME. A practical Hand-Book of the Ancient Sculptures and Masterpieces of Greek Art in Rome. Every visitor who desires to understand the works of the ancient sculptors should visit the various Museums of Rome with this valuable little work as a companion. *Price 1 lira.*

THE HOLY CITY JERUSALEM. Its Topography, Walls, and Temples. A new light on an ancient subject. Should be read by all to whom the name of Jerusalem is attractive, and will be found a valuable companion to those visiting the Holy City. Bound in cloth. Illustrations, maps, and plans. *Price 3 lire.*

This preservation copy
was printed and bound at
Bridgeport National Bindery, Inc.,
in compliance with U.S. copyright law.
The paper used meets the requirements
of ANSI/NISO Z39.48-1992
(Permanence of Paper).

C L R

2000